THE FATHER THEY WISH TO HAVE

The True Act of Human Fath... ...ation

"It is not flesh and blood but the heart which makes us fathers…"
–Johann Friedrich Von Schiller

[handwritten inscription: May God bless you and your family]

Faustinus U. Anyamele

Foreword by Bishop Joseph N. Perry J C L, Auxiliary Bishop of Archdiocese of Chicago

The Father They Wish to Have

The True Act of Human Fatherhood
and Its Consummation

*The Original Conception of True Human Fatherhood as Emanating
from the Participation in the Spirit of the Supreme Fatherhood of God*

Nihil Obstat: David Uebbing, M.A.
 Censor Liborum

Imprimatur: †Most Reverend Samuel J. Aquila, S.T.L.
 Archbishop of Denver
 January 14, 2014

The Father They Wish to Have:
The True Act of Human Fatherhood and Its Consummation
Copyright © 2014 **Faustinus U. Anyamele**
Catholic Archdiocese of Denver

ISBN: **1490340653**
ISBN 13: **9781490340654**
Library of Congress Control Number: **2013910304**
CreateSpace Independent Publishing Platform
North Charleston, South Carolina

In memory of my father, Ambrose Anyamele Okoroafor, who graciously lived so that I may experience the true nature and dignity of his human fatherhood, and a thank you to my uncle, Rev. Father Damian Oparah, who remains a father to this day.

Contents

ACKNOWLEDGMENTS

I give thanks to God, for granting me the grace, inspiration and courage to write this book. My sincere gratitude goes to Mary Huwa, who offered her time and energy in the early stages of this book. I want to thank her for the encouragement, support, and time she invested in reading and commenting on the book in its draft format.

My profound thanks to David Hicks (author, editor and lecturer at Regis University), who graciously shared his time and writing experience by providing useful feedback.

My deepest gratitude to Most Rev. Joseph N. Perry JCL, the Auxiliary Bishop of the Archdiocese of Chicago, for carefully reading this book and writing the Foreword, which was a great privilege.

Thanks to Most Rev. Charles J. Chaput, the Archbishop of Philadelphia, for his encouragement and support; to Most Rev. James D. Conley, the Bishop of Lincoln, for his inspiration and encouragement; and to my Archbishop, Most Rev. Samuel J. Aquila, Archbishop of Denver, for his service and leadership.

Also, my sincere appreciation and thanks are extended to Elizabeth Walker, Ph.D., Clinical Psychologist, and Gerry Doran, Ph.D., licensed Psychologist, who invested their time reading this book and providing professional feedback based on their experience and knowledge of fathers and families. I am honored by their endorsement.

I also offer my thanks to the many people who have encouraged and supported the creation of this book for many months, especially Jim and Suzanne Broski, Dennis and Norma Powers, Todd and Lindsay Filsinger, Dr. Bob and Dr. Mary Blattner, Joseph and Frances Yuknas, Gerry and Maureen Hayes, Ann Obrzut, Kyle and Chris West, John and Barbara Roessig, Michael and Puala McDermott, Ken and Pat Schultz, George and Cathy Brogan, Rick and Kathy Runyan, Dr. Mike and Lisa Harkabus, Andrew and LuAnn Silva, Mary Reis, George and Carolyn Brown, Dr. Maurice and Marianne Lyons, Anne Thomas, Susan Payne, Teresa Prochazaka, Dr. and Deacon John and Barb Volk, Vincent and Bernadine Zagarella, Dr. Richard and Mary Kemme, late Elizabeth Giordano, Mike and Yon Kramer, Christina Kramer, Jim and Patti Hanegan, Late Glenn K. Hanegan, Dr. Tom and Dorothy Peterson, Dr. Andy and Emily Achziger, Dr. Anthony Lilles, and David Uebbing, Chancellor of the Archdiocese of Denver.

Acknowledgments

This book would not have been possible without the fatherly love and presence of my uncle, Rev. Fr. Damian Oparah; the love of my mother, Magdaline Anyamele; my aunt, Rosaline Oparah and my siblings; the Anyamele-Okoroafor family; the Oparah family; and the many others who believe that fathers are most effective and beneficial to their children, when they embrace the idea that true human fatherhood is a reflection of the Divine Fatherhood of God.

FOREWORD

At a time when modernity insists on redefining the foundational institution of marriage and family to include same-sex marriage and parenting, Faustinus Anyamele has set forth, through his own Christian reflection, conjoined with that of respected authors and theologians, some of the best sentiments about human fatherhood. He has done so through a lens of the universal desire for the leadership of that one man whom generations have found singular with nourishing direction and counsel within an abiding relationship of affection and care.

Heretofore, society has not found a substitute for him even amid contemporary experimentation with sexual roles and the oft-commented-upon fragile nature of the marital state. This book will enlighten the reader with yet untapped sources of inspiration for human fatherhood in the Christian tradition.

Bishop Joseph N. Perry
Archdiocese of Chicago

Preface

In the late spring of 2008, as the birds sang of the promise of summer and the bees hovered over the blooming flowers looking for nectar—in the midst of this desirable, joyful season—I was left with a hurting child who remained in his own world, which I could not explain. I was sharing with a group of children the profound meaning of one of the commandments of God—"honor your father and your mother"—when an incident occurred that left me awestruck. It came in the form of an utterance from a child.

"We have to listen to our fathers and mothers when they instruct us on how to behave well or advise us to take or not take a particular action," I said, and as I spoke, a young child looked calmly into my eyes. I had the feeling that he was trying to extract something from me. "Do you understand what I am trying to say?" I asked the children, and, in unison, they said yes while nodding their heads—except for this one boy. I asked him directly, "Do you understand me?"

"Yes, Father," he said. "But I don't have a father." At those words, the whole room was reduced to silence, and the children's faces grew sad and sympathetic.

I paused. Time seemed to pass quickly. *Why does this child think that he has no father? What effect has this absence had in his young life?* I wondered.

"We all have fathers," I said. "For some, fathers are living and present; for others, fathers are living but far away; for still others, fathers are in heaven with God. But we all have fathers."

He looked at me with those blue eyes as if he were telling me I didn't understand. "I don't have a father," he said. "If I had a father, he would pick me up from school, take me to games, give me gifts, read to me at night, hear my stories, and take care of my mom and me. I only have my mom, and she told me she does not know anything about my father's whereabouts. She said my father left a long time ago with someone else. I don't know him, he doesn't know me, he does not visit me, and he does not give me any birthday gifts. I don't know what to say when my friends talk about their own fathers, because I don't have one; I only have my mom." With these words and the expression on his face, I could read his heart. Sadness had engulfed the being and the world of this child.

Never before had I felt so much guilt. First of all, in contrast to this child, I had the privilege of experiencing a father who loved my siblings and me, a father who was present at all times to watch us grow up and who had sacrificed much to make us happy, while cherishing and loving my mother. Even when death suddenly took him away from us when I was young, my maternal uncle, Father Damian Oparah, immediately became a father figure to my siblings and me. My uncle was compelled not by societal norms, conventional ideology, or cultural sentiment but simply goodwill and Christian charity; he stepped into our lives, became a father to us, and remains one to this day.

Secondly, I was unable to come up with any plausible answers for this child. Because of the sadness I saw in those innocent eyes, I felt compelled to come up with something to say that would give him a glimpse of hope. I started searching for a way to convince him that he had a father, in order to bring some consolation to his little heart. However, since I was unable to instantly produce a physical father for him, nothing I could have said would have made any sense to him. My philosophical or theological knowledge would not have gone very far in helping the situation, for he would not have understood the idea of filling the void created by a human father's absence with the divine Fatherhood of God.

It was then that it became clear to me that life's realities can sometimes become so much larger than philosophy, psychology, logic, and even theology. It was not the time for preaching or counseling; rather, it was the time to tell this young child with certainty that he did indeed have a father and to indicate where his father was.

What would you have said to this child? Would you have told him to ask his mother? His mother did not know anything about his father or his father's whereabouts, according to the child. Would you have told him he could replace his earthly father's absence with the divine presence of God the Father? That would be too big of a bite for him to chew at his age. I paused in sorrow as he gazed at me, awaiting my response. In his eyes I could see an innocent, hurting heart, and in this heart I could see the father he wished he had.

He wished for a father who would be a hero and a model he could look up to.

A father who would see his fatherhood as a divine vocation and carry it with sacredness. A father who would cherish and love the boy's mother and who would see his fatherhood through the femininity of his mother. A father who would be patient and watch him grow up. A father who would model himself in the spirit of the Fatherhood of the supreme God. A father who would be present and visible in both good and difficult times. A father who would lead by his servant-hood. A father whose love would be consistent and uninterrupted. A father who would help him when he was knocked down by life's realities or his human weaknesses. A father who would not shame him when he made mistakes but would forgive him, encourage him, and help bring out the best in him.

Feeling helpless, I put both of my hands on the child's shoulders, looked right into his piercing blue eyes, and said, "I am going to look for your father—that father that you wish you had. I will write him a letter, and I hope that after reading my letter he will one day come looking for you. He will then hold you close, console you when you are in pain, and wipe away the tears on your face when you hurt. He will play games with you, read for you at night before you go to sleep, take you to the park, and give you nice Christmas gifts. He will proudly call you *son*, and you will call him *father*; and when this happens, you can tell your friends in school about your father too."

"Do you promise?" he asked.

"Yes, I promise," I replied.

I do not know if that helped, but one thing I noticed was that his tight facial expression had relaxed. I had, however, just bound myself with a string of promises that I did not then know how to fulfill. I knew for certain that I did not know his father or where he lived. Nevertheless, I knew in my heart that someday, somehow, I would keep the promise that I had made to this young child to send a letter to his father.

This book is that letter. I hope his father reads it.

This is a letter to all fathers who are struggling to understand the essence of true human fatherhood and their roles as fathers. It is a letter that will help fathers who find themselves depriving their children of a true father's presence; it will help them rethink their decisions for the good of their children and for the true fulfillment of their own fatherhood. It is a letter that will help fathers understand the profound and complementary role of mothers in true human fatherhood. It is a letter that will spur fathers into a profound reflection on their actions and the consequences that their children might be left to bear when they are absent.

I hope it is a letter that will prompt fathers to take a moment to pause and reflect on the true meaning of the divine vocation of fatherhood and determine whether they have maintained a correspondence in the spirit of the ideal Fatherhood of God.

If any fathers determine that this is not so, this letter will help them set out in search of their children and be true fathers to them, no longer leaving them devoid of the affection of fathers but now providing them with models they can look up to and guides in their young lives. It is a letter that will help fathers carefully and prudently navigate to true fatherhood under the sad and heavy mist of a separation or a divorce. In addition, it is a letter that will help any father who was deprived of the presence of a true father in his own childhood, and it will provide practical help to him in dealing with his own potential or present fatherhood by directing him toward giving his own child or children what was denied him in his childhood.

This letter will encourage fathers to behold once more those young lives who are yearning for a true father and hungering for a father's love. "Children too are gifts from the Lord, the fruit of the womb, a reward."[1]

Finally, this is a letter of support and gratitude to fathers everywhere whose lives are a true testimony to that original conception of true fatherhood, a divine vocation.

CHAPTER ONE

You don't choose your family. They are
God's gift to you, as you are to them.
—Archbishop Desmond Tutu

The True Reason for the
Absence or Deprivation of Fathers

"The absence of a father causes psychological and moral imbalance and notable difficulties in family relationships,"[2] says Pope John Paul II. The phenomenon of the deprivation, absence, or lack of true presence of a father that results in single parenting has created a lot of psychological and emotional challenges for so many children in our society today and especially for those who are unable to find a true substitute to fill this void in their young lives.

In order to put this painful and regrettable reality into perspective, scholars of various human sciences (sociology, psychology, and the science of morality, for example) have, through analytic and evaluative methods, assembled empirical data to underscore the fact that "there is a 'father factor' in nearly all of the social problems facing America today."[3] The pains and tragedies that families and children have had to bear because fathers have neglected prenatal responsibilities, lacked true presence, and had dysfunctional relationships with their wives cannot be overemphasized. In the following, examples of data are provided that underscore the practical consequences of fathers walking away from the mothers of their children and sometimes abandoning their children in the process.

- Children in homes without fathers are almost four times more likely to be poor. In 2011, only 12 percent of children in married-couple families were living in poverty, compared with 44 percent of children in mother-only families.[4]

- Youths in households without fathers are still significantly more likely to be incarcerated than those in married-couple families. Youths who never had a father in the household are the most likely to be incarcerated.[5]

- Students living in homes without fathers are twice as likely to repeat a grade in school; only 10 percent of children living with both parents have ever repeated a grade, compared with 20 percent of children in families with stepfathers and 18 percent in mother-only families.[6]

Such statistics may not provide the complete picture of the painful reality, but they give us some idea of the ramifications of a father abandoning his children and depriving them of that divinely ordained dual complementarity of the presence of both a mother and a father. In this context, *complementarity* means, "first, that women and men share equally in the dignity proper to human persons, and second, that gender-specific differences between women and men are the basis for natural gifts or aptitudes that together contribute to human flourishing."[7] Thus, gender diversity in human nature should not be a cause for competition or inequality with regard to the events of life or practical human reality. Rather, it is a divine and natural necessity that gives meaning to human nature, because through their gender-specific differences man and woman complete each other by offering their inherent capability as a gift of love. Truly, adhering to this gender diversity brings also diverse functionality that promotes a healthy human growth and dignity. Hence, from the onset it was to be that the cooperation of a father and a mother would create a healthy family environment for the well-being of children.

I was once assigned to pastoral duty that entailed working with young students whose schooling ranged from preschool to eighth grade. I visited the students regularly and spent ample time with them. One fascinating aspect of this work was my experience of the innocent dynamism and uncensored developing personalities of these young children. You could easily spot the comic ones, the analytical ones, the assertive ones, and the free-minded ones. What made it so beautiful was that these children just lived out their different personalities uncensored and were unafraid of criticism; they were very authentic. The personality of one girl, named Lucy, was like a bold sign; you could read it from a distance. She was a healthy extrovert. She always wore a beautiful smile and was very friendly; when she saw someone, she greeted him or her loudly and asked how he or she was doing. Then she would overwhelm that person with a barrage of intelligent questions. I could see that she was well loved among her peers and very comfortable with the person she was.

Sadly for young Lucy, however, the tragedy of her parents' looming divorce began to take an emotional and psychological toll on her. I witnessed firsthand her devolution from a happy, energetic girl to a deeply despondent one. Not knowing what was happening at first, I was baffled by the degree of her emotional change and the extent to which she was diverted from being the person she was meant to be, to one she was forced to become. Lucy's family situation came to the attention of her teacher when Lucy began to miss her homework assignments and become disinterested in the class or class activities, which on several occasions landed her in the principal's office. The most painful experience for Lucy, according to her teacher, was when she overheard her father telling her mother that he was leaving her, that he didn't love her anymore, that they were getting a divorce, and that he was moving out of the state.

Lucy was emotionally affected because she understood that she might be denied her father's love and presence. She believed that if both parents brought her into the world, she was inalienably entitled to have both parents, who should become to her a visible sign of the nature of true love, equally love her, care for her, and remain fully present in her life, unabridged. Another, painful aspect of Lucy's experience was initially her feeling of helplessness; she could not keep her father from leaving or keep the divorce from happening. This feeling slowly but surely turned into an internal anger and fear of the unknown and what the future held for her. This began to affect her young psyche and her day-to-day activities. Sometimes such effects can push the lives of children like Lucy to unimaginable ruin.

Sadly, her parents went through with their divorce, and her father left for a different state.

When a father is thinking of abandoning his wife and children for one reason or another, he should be aware of the statistics given above. Such statistics do not in any way diminish the roles of mothers in children's lives or the hard work of so many mothers who have given their all and sacrificed so much while taking great care of their children in the absence of fathers so that these children could grow up to become happy and healthy members of society. Rather, the statistics expose the reasons behind what James Herzog calls the "father-hunger"[8] in children of our time and the tragedy of fathers neglecting responsibility.

In the Genesis account of the creation of human gender, God is said to have created man and then said, "I will make a suitable partner for him."[9] This "suitable partner" would be co-creator and nurturer of new life through love. This is the profound partnership or dual stewardship that God intended for us. When a father abandons this partnership, leaving the care of children to the mother alone and taking the status of a *visiting father* (partial presence) or an absent father, the children are the ones who suffer the greatest consequences, as we saw in Lucy's case. They are deprived of their natural right of a father's true presence.

Except in cases of abuse and child endangerment, most mothers will tell you that it is not an easy situation for them when the father's role in the life of his child is reduced so that he takes on the status of a *visiting father*. In some cases, the father intentionally leaves all responsibilities for the child's care solely to the mother, which makes the child's deprivation of that father's presence inevitable. In certain exceptional cases, the father (or, in rare cases, the mother) is prescribed a visitation schedule by the court, which may lead to a father's *partial presence* or *reluctant presence*. (However, as I will explain in chapter 5, there are still fathers who, even under the constraints of court-prescribed visitation agreements, remain truly committed and continually present in the lives of their children.)

Therefore, it is essential that the child should live and grow up in the continual physical presence of both a mother and a father. It is in this continual presence that the mutual parental love, which was the cause of their union and the new fruition of life, is made visible, and it is through this visibility that the child can become a witness to that love and understand what a true family is conceived to be. "Their parental love is called to become for the children the visible sign of the very love of God, from whom every family in heaven and on earth is named."[10] In essence, the absence of either one creates a vacuum of love in the child's life. Sometimes the vacuum is never filled. Other times, sadly, it is filled by an inappropriate or negative presence. In any case, the vacuum caused by the father's absence consciously or unconsciously has an adverse effect on the life of the child. Despite our understanding of this effect, however, the number of two-parent households continues to decline, while the number of single-parent households continues to increase.

The statistics cited at the beginning of this chapter reveal a reality that is problematic and saddening; however, they fail to provide honest and substantive answers to the core problem of the absence of fathers, and they do not reveal the main reason for why such a problem exists and only continues to get worse. Despite numerous studies, analyses, and evaluations of this issue, the true cause seems to have eluded us. We have focused squarely on social, economic, cultural, psychological, environmental, legal, and constitutional reasons and have therefore presumed that the adverse effect of the absence or deprivation of fathers can be fixed merely by enforcing child support (sometimes at a distance) or welfare programs or by hiring good legal advocates.

The National Fatherhood Initiative (NFI) and similar programs have brought awareness of the need for a father to play a positive role in the life of his family. But despite all the good intentions of these programs, they have not yet addressed the true reason for the persistence of the phenomenon of the absence and deprivation of fathers, and therefore there is still more to do to achieve the goal of helping fathers come to honest understandings of their *vocational* roles as *stewards to new life* and of the necessity that they become fully present in the lives of their children in order to ensure their well-being. We seem unready yet to confront the truth or call the problem by its name, which is as follows: over the course of time, the practice of human fatherhood has continued to drift further and further from its source—its origin—of true vitality, which is, for Christians as well as some non-Christians (who sympathize with true Christian life), *the supreme Fatherhood of God.*

In addition, it is also evident that, in our present cultures, there is an increased rejection of the traditional gender roles in marriage and parenting, which suggest that there are some things that men and women should do with the common goal of perfecting or complementing each other's existence. Some factions of the feminist movement have taken the feminist ideology (which may be beneficial with regard to certain aspects of human rights, equality, and the preservation of the dignity of both genders) to the extreme of being indifferent to, or totally rejecting, the value of fatherhood in the traditional human family; indeed, in *The Dialectic of Sex: The Case for Feminist Revolution*, Shulamith Firestone defines the woman's interest as contrary to that of the man's rather than complementary.

This thinking may have been triggered by an overdue frustration with a long history of patriarchal governance and societal and economic structuring that has created a chasm of inequality between men and women that is so deep in some parts of the world that human dignity and human rights have been compromised—which is contrary to the divine teachings of Christ. Presumably, this frustration prompted feminists like Jeffner Allen to write, "until patriarchy no longer exists, all females, as historical beings, must resist, rebel against, and avoid producing for the sake of men."[11] These kinds of ideologies have also cast great shadows of misunderstanding and misinterpretation on the true meaning of the traditional human family structure and on the roles of fathers and mothers in relation to their children.

The solution to the problem of the absence of fathers will keep eluding us until we are ready to take in the following truth: "The further a being is distant from that which is Being of itself, namely God; the nearer it is to nothingness. But the nearer a being stands to God, the further away it is from nothingness."[12] The more we walk in the presence of God and allow our human lives to be guided by his divine ordinances, the more we find meaning in our creation and joy in our vocation. However, the moment we take the journey of life without the guidance and ordinances of the author of life–God, we become disenchanted with life itself and the purpose of our creation. Our Lord Jesus Christ revealed this truth when he said, "Whoever remains in me and I in him will bear much fruit, because without me you can do nothing."[13] Therefore, once this connection between the human and the divine is severed, whether because of an act of free will or our culpable ignorance or sin, we begin to lose the meaning of our humanity and our divine vocation as well as an understanding of the true purpose behind our creation. In other words, only when we remain grafted to God (who is being-in-itself and the source of our being) and to our vocation (human fatherhood) do virtuous things begin to happen through us, and our vocation begins to bear fruit through our love for God and one another.

No program, human law, or governmental enforcement agency, no matter how good its intentions, would be able to restore true human fatherhood to our children or our society. Therefore, as long as we are unwilling to truly acknowledge the source and origin of our human fatherhood—God—any program and enforcement introduced, as remedies will only alleviate some of the burdens while leaving the core of the problem untouched. Saint Paul made the same truth known to the Ephesians when he wrote, "I bow my knee before the Father from whom every family in heaven and on earth is named."[14] In J. Scott Lidgett's analysis of this passage, he states, "Earthly fatherhood is, according to St. Paul, not the reality from which the divine Fatherhood is metaphorically derived. The opposite is true. God alone originally realizes the perfect ideal of fatherhood, and His Fatherhood is the original of which every other fatherhood is a shadow, and from which it derives its limited reality."[15] In this case, human fatherhood is not a human product or a product of society, and it is not biologically infused in humanity. Rather, it is a true answer to an invitation to participate in the spirit of the supreme Fatherhood of God as revealed by Christ; therefore, it is a divine vocation.

This participation is in relation to a new gift of life from the same God; this means that the Fatherhood of God as revealed in the life of Jesus Christ should become a model for the ideals of human fatherhood. Hence, human fatherhood cannot achieve its true nature on its own in isolation from the divine Fatherhood of God. The Fatherhood of God is the anchor that adheres us to the bedrock of truth because for us humans to act virtuously we need divine grace.

The further a man's fatherhood continues to drift from its source and origin, the more diminished his view of human fatherhood as a divine vocation becomes; instead he sees it as a mere socially, culturally, or biologically imposed responsibility that is enforced by human laws. These limited perspectives in effect rob from him the true meaning of being a father, making him feel that his role in caring for another life is forced upon him as an inconvenient responsibility that takes away his freedom and livelihood. The effect of such a mind-set in some fathers is the constant misunderstanding of the role of a father in a family and the distortion of the meaning of a human family as a divine gift of God. It also deters a couple from viewing a child as a gift and as "the living image of their love...the living and indissoluble concrete expression of their paternity and maternity."[16] For this reason, many children in this postmodern era are deprived of the human right of "dual parental care and love." According to the US Census Bureau, "over 24 million children live apart from their biological fathers. That is one out of every three children in America."[17] Indeed, many have no one to call father, and in certain cases, sadly, some have no family at all. In addition, the inevitable consequence of an unstable family is an unstable society and a lack of harmony in the world.

In its 1993 address on the World Day of Peace, the Vatican, under the guidance of John Paul II, stated, "Many, too many children are deprived of the warmth of a family. Sometimes the family is absent: in fact, the parents, taken up by other interests, leave their children to their own devices. In other cases, the family simply does not exist."[18] It is every child's inalienable right to have *a father* and *a mother* and live in *a family.* No child should be deprived of any of these three human elements (a father, a mother, and a family) that are essential to life. For these reasons, no condition provides justification for any father to deny his child that divine gift of his fatherhood, his fatherly presence, and his fatherly love.

In our society, some Christians rarely take cognizance of a truth that is self-evident in our origins: that human fatherhood (like human motherhood) is ordained by God as a vocation that has one principal goal, and that goal is to do the will of God. The pursuit of and dedication to this vocation becomes, through the grace of God, an instrument of a father or mother's salvation. According to the Genesis account of creation, "God created man in his image; in the divine image He created him; male and female he created them. God blessed them, saying to them: Be fertile and multiple; fill the earth and subdue it."[19] In this account of creation, God created, commanded, and commissioned humanity, inviting it to be a partner with him in his divine continual creation of sacred human life. Our acceptance of this invitation means we must freely enter into the covenant of holy matrimony, which is an effect of love and self-giving. In this divine union, the love that germinates through this *true self-giving* becomes flesh in the procreation and nurturing of new life.

Therefore, human fatherhood *is not our own*; rather, it emanates from the one supreme Fatherhood of God. In essence, we will one day render an accountability of our human fatherhood before the supreme Fatherhood of God, to whom Fatherhood is an act of being; it belongs to him and is original to his existence, while human fatherhood comes to us through our true participation in the spirit of this One Fatherhood of God, designed to be mastered through grace, which elucidates our human dependency on the divine.

CHAPTER TWO

One night a father overheard his son pray:
"Dear God, make me the kind of man my daddy is."
Later that night the father prayed:
"Dear God, make me the kind of man my son wants me to be."
—Unknown

True Human Fatherhood

Christians (and some non-Christians) believe that the only subject that reveals its meaning by its very existence— and that is permanent, ideal, perfect, and true—is God. As Joseph MacDowell and Thomas Williams write, "Without God as the bedrock absolute, all possibility of objective truth collapses. Those who deny God must resign themselves to believing in an accidental, mechanistic universe devoid of truth, meaning, destiny, or purpose, or they must accept a world of illusion and uncertainty about reality itself."[20] According to this, accepting the truth implies accepting that every perfection and truth emanates from God, who is the bedrock of our lives and world and the only absolute truth. Some modern thinkers may object to these premises as leaning toward theological absolutism, but we cannot deny our constant yearning for absolute truth.

There is this internal desire in every human person for that which is certain or absolute on the face of a world in flux. "At the center of the human heart is the longing for an absolute truth and goodness, a longing which is always there and is never appeased by any object in this world."[21] Since no object in this finite world is the bedrock of certainty or truth, we have no other option than to look elsewhere for absolute truth, certainty, or goodness, for Christians find that in God. Therefore, when someone asserts that a father's relationship with his child is "good," or "true," our response should be, in relation or comparison to what is this judgment being made?

Inevitably, in trying to understand *true human fatherhood*, we have to reference the bedrock of truth or the source from which all human fatherhood emanates—God. First, however, we should determine what the meaning of the term *fatherhood* is as it is attributed to humans. Second, we should ask why humans are even addressed as fathers, given that our Lord Jesus Christ emphatically proclaimed in the Gospel of

Matthew, "Call no man your father on earth, for you have one Father, who is in heaven" (3:27). Third, on a more critical note, we should ask if true human fatherhood is even attainable. Is it instead what Alfred North Whitehead refers to as a "hopeless quest"?

MEANING OF THE TERM FATHER

According to the *Oxford American Dictionary*, the word *father* means, first, *a man's relationship to his natural (biological) child.* It also means *a man who has continuous care of a child.* In this definition, there are dual and complementary meanings of the word *father*: (1) a male who begot or engendered a child naturally (biologically) through a sexual complementarity with a woman and (2) a male who consistently cares for, educates, and protects a child. In my view, the latter meaning can stand on its own without the former, while the former meaning should never stand on its own without the latter.

This implies that a father could be a male who protects and is also continually present with and cares for a child without sharing any kind of a biological link or relationship with him or her (e.g., when a man adopts a child or acts as a child's father figure); having a natural or a biological relationship with a child, on the other hand, inevitably incurs the responsibility for caring, protecting, and being continually present for the engendered child. It is like a package in which two elements are wrapped together: unwrapping the first element consequentially means unwrapping the second.

Notably, it is true that not all sexually potent men have the emotional capacity or interest to follow through with raising a child they biologically sired and providing the nurturing and guidance he or she needs to reach maturity. Therefore, I believe that a man (or a woman, for that matter) should not biologically engender a child without being emotionally ready and willing to accept responsibility for nurturing the child and remaining a true presence in his or her life; failing to abide by this universal principle would be a disservice to the humanity of the engendered child, the human race in general, and God, who is the author of all human life.

Sadly, the world and our society have taught us that we have the freedom and potential to separate the two elements (that is, the biological engendering of a child and the continuous care of him or her). However, we have to understand that freedom and potential do not necessarily translate to justification. Just because I can do something or am free to do something does not in any way justify the action as morally right, naturally acceptable, or representative of true human behavior. Because so many fathers have lived out the first definition of fatherhood without the complement of the second, that divinely intended family structure wherein a father and a mother remain truly present with their child in complementarity has deteriorated. This act of *selective fatherhood* has created an existential (psychological, moral, spiritual, social, economic, and academic) deficit for so many of our children today, and in most cases, these children are forced into a complex world without all the necessary skills and tools to deal with its challenges.

For instance, when a father (who should be, along with the mother, the first and true teacher of the child) decides to abandon his natural responsibility to his child and leaves the mother alone to care for him or her, he denies his child the unique practical knowledge that only he can supply as a father. (Likewise, the mother can provide practical knowledge only from her own uniqueness and natural aptitude as a mother.) Therefore, in the heart and person of the child whose father is not present, the father's own natural space is desolate because he is not available. Upon stepping onto the world's stage, this child will be confronted with something he or she has never experienced, learned, or even conceptualized, and that can be challenging and frustrating and cause emotional and psychological problems that may affect his or her development into a healthy adult. As a result, the child could begin to desperately search for that which was denied: a true father figure.

In some cases, the child might be fortunate to find that father figure in a stepfather, uncle, guardian, teacher, or coach. In other cases, the child could fall into the wrong hands, which may lead to ruin; the child's good intentions could be thwarted by a father figure's behavior or by the child's own misguided (and perhaps desperate) needs, and the end product of his or her relationship with a father figure may be quite disappointing or even disastrous to the child's well-being. Sadly, this may also be true in the child's relationship with a biological father who is compromised and not living out his true and divinely ordained vocation.

Therefore, when the word *father* is used, it is meant to connote one who not only engenders or adopts a child but also continually cares for, educates, and protects that which has been engendered or adopted. To be clear, the terms *continually cares for* and *protects* are not synonymous with control, dominance, or obsession with authority. Rather, they are synonymous with love, freedom, selfless service, encouragement, appropriate praising and reprimanding, education, prudence, patience, insight, inspiration, understanding, dialogue, and the transmission of true knowledge about God and humanity.

Any healthy male human who is not sexually impotent or impeded by other medical or genetic issues can biologically beget a child. Sadly, even through rape and sexual abuse (profoundly immoral and depraved acts), a child can be engendered. So, does the biological element alone constitute true fatherhood? I agree with Karol Wojtyla, who unequivocally says no: "A human being is a person, so that the simple natural fact of becoming a father or a mother has deeper significance, not merely a biological but also a personal significance. Inevitably, it has profound effects upon the 'interior' of a person, which are summarized in the concept of parenthood."[22] In essence, the biological act of begetting a child does not, on its own, cause one to become a true father. Rather, the subsequent *caring action* in relation to the engendered child is what defines true human fatherhood. This absorption of human fatherhood in the spirit of the divine Fatherhood of God (as revealed by Christ) is based on the male human's ability to harness those innate characteristics of divine love endowed by the creator and apply them to the practical or existential reality of a relationship with a child. This very truth prompted Johann Friedrich Von

Schiller to say that "it is not flesh and blood but the heart which makes us fathers..."

WHY ARE HUMANS CALLED FATHERS?

Should humans be addressed as fathers? What does our Lord Jesus Christ imply by asking us not to call any man a father in this temporal world?

For our Lord Jesus Christ, the only subject capable of carrying within itself its own fatherhood is God, which means that divine Fatherhood endures in the nature of God. We Christians believe that God caused human fatherhood in order to incorporate the male gender (like the female gender) in his act of divine caring for humankind; therefore, true human fatherhood owes its origin to the divine Fatherhood of God. So for our Lord Jesus Christ, God is the author of fatherhood; it belongs to him alone, and no person has the right to claim it for himself. However, out of divine privilege, humans are called to the *vocation of fatherhood* by participation in the act modeled by God the Father through Christ. So humans are capable of becoming fathers and can be addressed as fathers not as a natural prerogative but as a status of divine privilege in the context of true imitation of the author of all true human fatherhood, God.

IS TRUE HUMAN FATHERHOOD ATTAINABLE?

True human fatherhood is not a "hopeless quest" but an attainable quest insofar as we come to the self-evident truth that its attainability is both divine and human—which implies that true human fatherhood is fully attainable only by imitation and consummation in the spirit of the divine Fatherhood of God. These acts of true imitation and consummation are within our reach if humans could submit their fatherhood to the guidance of the following truths.

My human fatherhood originates from God.

My human fatherhood is a divine vocation.

My human fatherhood does not belong to me.

The one goal of my human fatherhood is to do the will of God.

1. GOD THE FATHER IS THE ONE AND ONLY SOURCE AND ORIGIN OF OUR HUMAN FATHERHOOD

During the medieval, or scholastic, era, Saint Thomas Aquinas, in an effort to bring some clarity to the *law of causality* (a fundamental truth that everything has a cause), argued that every finite thing receives its existence from another, and that God is the *necessary being* (first cause) from which every other thing begins to exist. Through his formulation of *contingency,* he went further to explain that, in nature, plants and animals are finite beings—they come into existence and then stop existing with time. The fact that these finite life forms can cease to exist implies that there must have been a moment in which nothing ever existed, and that makes it difficult to account for the source of all finite things. "Therefore," he writes, "if at one time nothing was in existence, it would have been impossible for anything to have begun to exist; and thus even now nothing would be in existence—which is absurd."[23] The logical truth here is that the existence of these finite life-forms is insufficient to account for the existence of other finite life-forms, because they don't carry within themselves their own existence (i.e., they do not cause themselves or create themselves); in other words, the finite beings are the result of causes or of a single cause.

Hence, that *necessary cause (a being that causes itself)* that is responsible for the existence of this finite thing must be a subject whose nature is *to be*, and it does not need to be caused by another or even begin to exist; rather, it has always existed and is absolute, eternal, and infinite. Aquinas continues, "Therefore we cannot but postulate the existence of some being having of itself its own necessity, and not receive it from another, but rather causing in others their necessity. This all men speak of as God."[24] In other words, according to our human experience, everything in this present world is caused by another or owes its coming into existence to another existing thing. There must be an origin that set off this whole chain of causes and effects (the first cause); that is what Christians believe God to be.

This formulation and clarification of the law of causality took Holy Scripture as its root—specifically, the Genesis account of creation, which asserts that, in the beginning, God made the universe and its contents out of nothing. This is referred to as *creatio ex nihilo* (Gen. 1:1). Hence, human life is the effect of God's infinite love, and human fatherhood (and motherhood) is the effect of a new human life. Thus, God intended from the beginning to enter into a partnership with humanity through a commission that carries within itself a level of responsibility before God.

Through this very act of divine creation and commission to humanity (to continue reproducing the same divine gift of life, which God extended to humanity out of his love) comes the birth and institution of the human family. The Pastoral Constitution of the Church in the Modern World, states; "Wishing to associate them in a special way with his own creative work, God blessed man and woman with the words: 'Be fruitful and multiply' (Gen. 1:28). The spouses would cooperate generously with love of the Creator and Savior, who through them will in due time increase and enrich His family."[25] The same divine gift of love to humanity becomes incarnate in the new fruit of a begotten human life, as illustrated in this diagram:

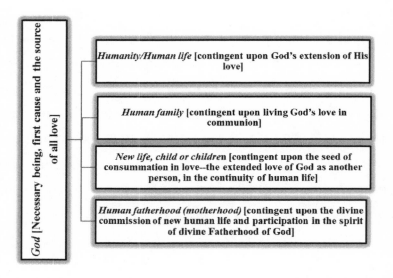

The Divine Inherent in Humanity and Human Fatherhood

We can see from the diagram how inherent God is in our humanity; all things occur or exist through him. He made us, and we belong to him, together with every effect that proceeds from our nature and existence.

Therefore, these commissions of *fruitfulness* and *multiplication* established new dual roles for humanity, fatherhood, and motherhood, and these roles are described as coming into existence only in their relationship with the fruit of new life. Both males and females were endowed with the essence of God as procreators of sacred life and invited to be partners with God in extending this divine gift of human life. "Thus the couple, while giving themselves to one another, give not just themselves but also the reality of children, who are a living reflection of their love, a permanent sign of conjugal unity and a living and inseparable synthesis of their being father and a mother."[26] The male acceptance of this partnership opens the door to participation in the spirit of the supreme Fatherhood of God. Once we acknowledge this divine and existential truth—that God is the cause of our human fatherhood—we will have taken the first step in a journey of many steps toward attaining true human fatherhood.

2. OUR HUMAN FATHERHOOD IS A DIVINE VOCATION

"Called to give life, spouses share in the creative power and fatherhood of God."[27] To grasp the profundity of human fatherhood as a call or vocation, let us first look at the meaning of *vocation*. Despite the continued use of the word *vocation* to designate a professional career, it was first used in the fifteenth century in a Christian context to refer to a divine call to the service of humankind.[28] One does not choose a vocation for oneself; rather, one willingly and obediently responds to a summon initiated by the one who calls, a "voice" that is not confined in our human nature but echoes internally in our human hearts, souls, and minds, calling us to serve God. Therefore, in a Christian context, every divine vocation is commissioned to serve a cause greater than one's humanity.

Every divine vocation taken up must coincide with the plan of God, which means that the goal of any divine commission must cohere with the divine plan and intention of God. When one is summoned or called by God, one is called to a divine mission of love and for love, to be an instrument extending the pure divine love of God; this is also true of the vocation of fatherhood. "The conjugal relationship makes a man and a woman intermediaries in the transmission of life to a new human being. Because they are persons, they take part consciously in the work of creation (*procreation*), and from this point of view are *participes creatoris* [participants in creation]."[29] This implies that God wished for man and woman to reign, govern, lead, nurture, and protect his creation. He commissioned each according to his or her sexuality, functionality, ability, and talent. The woman's vocation complements the man's, and the man's vocation complements the woman's; "[God] affirmed that 'alone' man does

not completely realize this essence. He realizes it only by existing 'with someone' — and even more deeply and completely —
by existing 'for someone.'"[30]

So God's call to the human person to be a partner in the
extension of his gift of life and love is a call or vocation that
comes to complete realization only in communion, not in isolation or solitude. A man, in complementary union with a
woman with whom he is in love, is called to cooperate with
God in the transmission of life, which guarantees the continuity
of the human family. In this divine invitation, both genders are
fashioned in the same nature but with diverse functionalities or
roles as they act jointly with God in his act of human creation
and nurturing.

Reflecting on the diverse functional roles that God gave
to both man and woman, Archbishop Fulton J. Sheen writes,
"The man governs the home, but the woman reigns."[31] From
this perspective, one may say that God commissioned woman
thusly: "You shall be the sanctuary of life. In your womb, I
shall reveal my glory and majesty. In your womb, I shall continue to manifest my love as in the beginning by giving flesh to
my essence, which is life. Although this life belongs to me, you
shall reign over it and be ever present in it. You shall naturally
be an extension of my love, and for this reason I shall join you

and your child together (symbolized by the umbilical cord) inseparably; you shall be a mother to this life not in isolation or solitude but in communion with a man."

One may also say that God similarly commissioned the man thusly: "You shall be the guardian of my essence—life—and by imitating my divine Fatherhood, you shall be an extension of my love to this life. You shall govern this life, protect this life, lead this life back to me, and be a father to this life not in isolation or solitude but in communion with a woman."

In her reigning, the mother gathers, nurtures, harmonizes, guides, and preserves new life, while, in his governing, the father leads, protects, and serves new life. Therefore, this interpretation does not unfavorably compare the differences in the roles of mother and father; rather, it provides a succinct exposition of the uniqueness of each one's functionality as both work toward one common goal.

The man is called to *govern* God's gift of life under the *reign* of the mother, and the woman is called to *reign* over this life under the *governance* of the father. Both the man and the woman were divinely and originally created to submit to each other for a common cause that transcends their humanity: the begetting of new life through love. It is the equivalent of dipping our human nature in the fount of divine mystery and being left in awe. For "both in the conception and in birth of a new child, parents find themselves face to face with a 'great mystery' (cf. Eph. 5:32)."[32]

In an effort to bring to clarity the comprehensive summary of this vocation of fatherhood, Pope John Paul II states the following in his apostolic exhortation *Familiaris consortio*:

> In revealing and in reliving on earth the very fatherhood of God, a man is called upon to ensure the harmonious and united development of all the members of the family; he will perform this task by exercising generous responsibility for the life conceived under the heart of the mother, by a more solicitous commitment to education, a task he shares with his wife, by work which is never a cause of division in the family but promotes its unity and stability, and by means of the witness he gives of an adult Christian life which effectively introduces the children into the living experience of Christ and the Church.[33]

Hence, the father, through his own example of an authentic Christian and ethical life, leads his child to God, their source and creator and the one who summoned and commissioned the father from the beginning. Therefore, a man is called to the vocation of human fatherhood by a new life (his child), and it is this new life, created by God, divine and sacred, that prompts the human vocation to fatherhood. Without it, true human fatherhood is nonexistent. The understanding of this truth is the second step in the journey of many steps to true human fatherhood.

3. OUR HUMAN FATHERHOOD DOES NOT BELONG TO US AND IS NOT CAUSED BY US BUT IS GIVEN

When we freely enter into a marriage that leads to the bringing of new life into the world, the resulting fatherhood is often thought of as originating from our free will and individual authorship or ownership. However, we have to understand that the God-given freedom to bring new life into the world is not equivalent with ownership or authorship of life. If a mother were to give her car keys to her son and grant him permission to drive her car, that does not mean that the car belongs to the son; when he uses the car, however, it will be his responsibility to make sure the car is used with care and that, at the end, it is safely accounted for. Therefore, the freedom to do a particular thing does not grant one ownership of that thing; rather, one is expected to exhibit responsibility, care, and accountability. This adds up to *stewardship*. Christians hold this to be true and believe that human fatherhood is a divine gift that comes directly from God; it is authored by him and him alone.

"No one can receive anything except what has been given him from heaven."[34] It would be absurd for us to claim ownership of anything, even human fatherhood, because it is not of our own making. Human fatherhood is given to us as a privilege that derives from answering the divine call of partnership in which a father becomes the steward of a new life that belongs to the *necessary cause*—God.

Once a man has engendered a new life through sexual complementarity with a woman and comes to understand that by virtue of his fatherhood he is solely a *steward* of new life, he takes the third step on his journey to true human fatherhood. Fundamentally, he realizes that his fatherhood is not an end in itself but a means to an end; in other words, he sees his human fatherhood as a ladder, both for himself and for his child, which they will climb as they aspire toward the divine Fatherhood of God. Hence, human fatherhood is divinely ordained to make the invisible God visible to our children; thus our children will begin to understand what it means to call God *Abba*, or *Father*.

4. OUR HUMAN FATHERHOOD IS ORDAINED TO BE SPENT IN DOING THE WILL OF GOD

Explaining the core purpose of human life to the understanding of his disciples, Christ taught the following: "For whoever wishes to save his life will lose it, but whoever loses his life for my sake will find it."[35] Christ is not asking us to reject our God-given gift of life or to set it on a fast track to annihilation. Rather, he is urging us to truly embrace and cherish the gift of life. Only then will we be able and willing to spend it in doing the will of the one to whom all life belongs.

For in spending our lives in servitude of the will of God, we bring it to fulfillment as God intended from the beginning. God invites humanity to participate in his creation so that we can carry out his will and intention: first, to reveal himself as he is in the person of our Lord Jesus Christ, who not only made the invisible God visible but revealed his unfathomable love, and second, that our wounded humanity (wounded, that is, from original sin) be reinstated, repaired, restored, and reconfigured through Christ and then be presented before God the Father so that we may remain in His divine love. Hence, by falling in love with God's plan of revealing himself and restoring our wounded humanity, the earthly father keeps alive in the heart of his child the divine, unquenchable flame of pure love.

Human fatherhood may be seen as a key that opens the door to the journey of the continuous transformation of that gift of new life—a father's child—according to the will of God through Christ. Therefore, in every step leading to the final step of the father's stewardship of new life, he should ask himself the following questions:

1. Is my fatherhood *revealing* and *reliving* the supreme Fatherhood of God while I lead my child to do the will of God?

2. Is my fatherhood a ladder that my child can trustfully climb with ease toward the supreme Fatherhood of God?

3. Am I manifesting a true earthly human fatherhood that emanates from the supreme Fatherhood of God so that my child can envision what it means to become a true earthly father to another new life through his or her own participation in the absolute ideal Fatherhood of God?

4. Is my child able to see God through my human fatherhood? If my child is a son, can he say he wants to be the kind of father his father is? If my child is a daughter, can she say she wants to marry a man who can be the kind of father her father is?

5. Am I demonstrating to my child how to live an authentic Christian life and remain in the love of God, which necessitates obedience and submission to the will of God?

Furthermore, could a non-Christian father be a true father to his child? The answer is "yes", because Christians believe that God does not discriminate or hold back his divine grace from those who express docility and receptivity; it is this grace that enables us to achieve virtuous acts in our lives, like true fatherhood, love, forgiveness, compassion, and justice. We believe that the divine ordinances of God are still written in the heart of every human being from the moment of creation prior to the writing of the Holy Scripture and the establishment of Christian religion. These divine ordinances remind us of, and guide us back to, the truth. (Over the course of human history, these divine laws, etched in our hearts, may have been distorted by sin, but Christ came into the world and restored what was broken, giving to all humankind a model to follow or imitate.) From these divine ordinances, etched in every human heart, flow true Christian values and morals that are virtuous and good and that form our human consciences.

To what can we compare the *true act* of human fatherhood? Imagine a painter who is about to grace her canvas with an image worthy of an original landscape that has the touch of nature and that was perfected by its creator. She picks up her paintbrush, dips it into the finest of paints of various colors, and makes just one stroke on the canvas. That one stroke of paint unfortunately does not bring to reality what she perceives for the very reason that the carbon copy of the original landscape she perceives and wishes to produce on the canvas is not original to her. Therefore, all of her artistic skills and ingenuities need to be put to use. She employs brush stroke after brush stroke, dot after dot, and line after line, erasing and replacing, fading and highlighting, sighing with dissatisfaction, and nodding her head in approval. She pours out her entire being, her skills, her visions, her talents, and her time.

Now she paints her joys and sorrows, her difficulties and pains, and her sadnesses and regrets. A sympathetic observer can see her entire life unfolding on a canvas and being made visible. At the end, she takes her work in its finest condition and places it side by side with the natural landscape, and she beams with satisfaction because the image on the canvas is now worthy of the original—the natural landscape. That work of art has become original to her, the child of her inspiration and perception and the product of her tireless efforts and hopes. She has become one with her unique and original work of art. You can identify her in her works, which can be differentiated from any other work of art by any other artist.

We have to remember that it was only after many strokes, lines, and dots were made and many colors were used that the painted landscape became worthy of the natural landscape. Conspicuously, as a good artist, she did not solely seek to replicate the natural landscape, but in a sincere effort of interpretation, she created her own original image worthy of the first original—the natural landscape. This can be equated to a true human fatherhood. Human fatherhood can never match the divine Fatherhood of God. However, seeing the divine Fatherhood of God (as demonstrated by Christ) as a superior and true model, the human father can begin to build, block by block, his own example of a true fatherhood modeled after the divine Fatherhood that was revealed by Christ.

Therefore, in molding true human fatherhood to the delight of his child and of God, a father has to be ready to pour out his entire being like a libation and demonstrate it through his unconditional love, pure patience, forgiveness, praises, and reprimands. He has to be willing to walk extra miles into the world of his child (while not forgetting the child is still a child), hold the child's hands, and begin a journey with him or her to the world of growth and maturity without sacrificing the child's natural spirit (which is forthright, credulous, natural, and unpretentious). In the father's attempt to interpret and imitate the divine model of Fatherhood (as revealed by Christ) through many virtuous acts, he will at the end present a fatherhood that is worthy of its original source—God.

Hence, begetting a child (whether biologically, spiritually, or by adoption) does not establish true fatherhood. These acts of begetting, engendering, and adopting are only the means to true human fatherhood, not ends in themselves. The end comes once human fatherhood has been brought to completion in the spirit and image of the Fatherhood of God. "Thus every element of human generation which is proper to man, and every element which is proper to woman, namely human *'fatherhood'* and *'motherhood,'* bears within itself a likeness to or analogy with the divine 'generating' and with that 'Fatherhood' which in God is 'totally different,' that is completely spiritual and divine in essence."[36] Every human act of generating another of its kind, is not a generation in isolation, rather it is a generation of a prototype (image of God) of the source of life—God. Therefore, every element that brings about true fatherhood (likewise motherhood) will always be traced back to God.

True human fatherhood inevitably needs to manifest different elements that are inspired by both humanity and the divine—the natural as well as the spiritual—in order to present itself as worthy of its source.

CHAPTER THREE

*The most important thing that a father
can do for his children is to love their mother.*
—*Theodore M. Hesburgh, CSC.*

*To father well, fathers must be…capable of fostering a loving bond
between themselves and their wives.*
—*John W. Miller*

The Woman's Role in True Human Fatherhood

Christians believe that the Holy Bible was written in human language with the divine inspiration of the Holy Spirit: "For no prophecy ever came through human will; but rather human beings moved by the Holy Spirit spoke under the influence of God."[37] Therefore, we hold these scriptural words to be true revelations of God's love and divine plan in human language. The author of the second account of creation in the book of Genesis described a complementarity of human femininity and human masculinity in a descriptive, figurative manner:

> The Lord God said: It is not good for the man to be alone. I will make a suitable partner for him. ...So the Lord God cast a deep sleep on the man, and while he was asleep, he took out one of his ribs and closed up its place with flesh. The Lord then built up into a woman the rib that He had taken from the man. When He brought her to the man, the man said: "This one, at last, is bone of my bone and flesh of my flesh; this one shall be called 'woman' for out of 'her man' this one has been taken." That is why a man leaves his father and mother and clings to his wife and the two of them become one body.[38]

This very passage can be interpreted as meaning that God put humanity to sleep ("the Lord God cast a deep sleep on the man") and that, after this divinely induced slumber, humanity woke up in the duality of male and female gender.[39] This human account of God's divine creation reveals the truth of a divinely ordained sexual complementarity, dependency, and equality that should exist in the human race. Human masculinity, then, may have meaning only in human femininity, and vice versa. That is why humanity "is marked by this primordial duality."[40]

This implies that the intention of God from the beginning was for man and woman to live in communion of love and not in isolation.

Also, the second account of human creation reveals an exclamation of happiness, fulfillment, and completeness on the part of the male gender; when he beholds the female gender — he assertively cries out in joy, affirming the oneness of their humanity ("... bone of my bone and flesh of my flesh) upon seeing a companion.[41] "Only the woman created from the same 'flesh' and cloaked in the same mystery, can give a future to the life of the man. It is therefore above all on the ontological level that this takes place, in the sense that God's creation of woman characterizes humanity as a relational reality."[42] From another perspective, this can be interpreted to mean that when God removed man's rib (a way of helping man realize his completeness in woman), man felt incomplete. For this very reason, man set out on an expedition in search of the fullness and completeness of his humanity, which he finally found in the woman that God brought to him.

One could assert, then, that the duality of the sexes gives meaning to the human race and at the same time reveals the intention of its divine maker: in its duality, humanity is called to a vocation of love, which is an extension of God's divine love. "Creating man and woman in his image...God inscribed in the humanity of man and woman the vocation, and thus the capacity and responsibility of love and communion."[43] In other words, man and woman were created and fashioned to live in companionship and not in isolation. Whether literally or exegetically interpreting this biblical passage, the meaning one comes to in the end is that *the complementary nature between a man and a woman is divinely intended.*

In this profound oneness of duality in the union of a man and a woman, grace and nature are commingled and mutually embraced; this relationship is what Catholics refer to as *sacramentum,* which means a profound mystery. It is something that we live out but cannot fully comprehend with our human intellect and senses[44]. As a man and a woman give themselves to each other, the two are no longer two but become one flesh, indivisible and indissoluble. "What therefore God has joined together let not man separate" (Matthew 19:6).

Christians believe that, according to the creative plan of God, a man should cling to his wife and be one with her, love her, cherish her, and uphold her dignity. In this way the man becomes a helper first, which encourages the woman, in her turn, to become a helper to the man. In other words both are divinely called to be helpers to each other. One aspect of the help of woman makes the continuity of humanity a reality: she is a helper who becomes the sanctuary of humanity, a sanctuary where the sacredness of life is fashioned by God the creator. Pope John Paul II, expanding beyond the meaning given in the book of Genesis, explained that the word *helper* in this context does not merely refer to someone who performs a particular human act; rather, it is an act of being.[45]

Hence what God intended by making both woman and man as helpers to each other was for them to serve the holistic role of bringing meaning to humanity; one aspect of this holistic role on the part of woman is that she does this by generating life through the help of the man, and both should be subsequently and continuously nurturing that generated life. As a "helper" to man, woman gives existential meaning to him (and vice versa) and becomes the sanctuary in which God may manifest his glory. It is also very important to note that even women who are not married or do not or cannot have children still bear and carry within themselves the obligation to act in their divine roles as *beings who complete humanity* and *sanctuaries of life for the continuity of humanity* by virtue of their sexuality and functionality---spiritual motherhood or motherhood by adoption.

> Motherhood involves a special communion with the mystery of life as it develops in the woman's womb...In the light of the 'beginning,' the mother accepts and loves as a person the child she is carrying in her womb. This unique contact with the new human being developing within her gives

rise to an attitude toward human beings—not only toward her own child, but every human being—which profoundly marks the woman's personality…The man—even with all his sharing in parenthood—always remains 'outside' the process of pregnancy and the baby's birth; in many ways, he has to learn his own 'fatherhood' from the mother.[46]

From conception through pregnancy and birth, a mother develops a *natural bond* with the child in her womb; this bond is biological, psychological, mysterious, and maternal because in her womb—in the midst of the physical burden of pregnancy—a life is being fashioned and nurtured. In pregnancy, women do everything to protect their children and keep them healthy; they sacrifice, and they bear almost unbearable pains. The burden of labor falls entirely on the pregnant woman (while, to be sure, the emotional aspect of the pregnancy and the pain of the mother's labor also affects the man who is awaiting the arrival of this new life), but she accepts it graciously, knowing that the sacredness and beauty of what is residing in her womb outweighs all the pains and agonies. The mother is biologically linked to her child as well as physically attached by the umbilical cord, and she is spiritually connected because she allows God to manifest and fashion his divine and sacred gift of life in her womb. The mother's womb becomes the sanctuary that welcomes and carries the sacred gift of life from God.

After birth comes the true maternal joy that heals all pain and anguish experienced during childbirth, for out of her a new gift of life has come forth. This child will suckle her breast and sleep in her tender arms. The man who begot or engendered this child with the mother and played a vital supporting role during the pregnancy will continue building his relationship with the child—a relationship that started from the moment he received the good news of conception—by participating in the fullness of the *natural* relationship between the mother and the child.

The maternity of the mother has opened the door to the fatherhood (the paternity) of the man. At the moment of delivery, the mother will say to the child, "Meet your father," and to the man, "Meet your child." "Fatherhood can occur only when a specific woman admits a specific man into the reproductive process and accords him a recognized status as father of her children. Fatherhood is thus not even possible apart from the willing deference and collaboration of a woman with a man."[47] Womanhood is the single key (in complementarity with the man) that opens the door to all human fatherhood, which means that human fatherhood can only become real when a particular woman willingly admits a particular man into the reproductive process that results in the generation of a new life.

In essence, the man's journey to true fatherhood begins through the femininity of the woman, even in a case of adoption. Participating in the natural mother-child relationship, the father will begin admiring the child, holding the child in his arms, feeding the child, comforting the child, and consoling the child in times of distress. He will wake up in the middle of the night to attend to the needs of the crying child, and while he patiently watches the young one grow, he will protect and care for him or her.

Through all these actions, the man starts sharing the burden and sacrifices involved in the nurturing of a new life, which the mother agrees to undertake from the moment of conception. The bond between mother and child is determined by nature because the child grows in her and she feels every inch of movement and every touch; she knows when something is not right, but the bond between father and child comes into existence by way of participation in the *natural* bond, which Peter J. Wilson refers to as the *primary bond* in his book *Man the Promising Primate: The Condition of Human Evolution.* This true participation of the father in the bond over time spurs in the child the internalization of the father's role.

A family friend once invited me over for dinner, and I was glad to honor their invitation. Upon my arrival, I witnessed an active and energetic family consisting of a young couple and their three-year-old son. While I was talking with the father over a glass of wine—his wife moved between the living room and the kitchen to keep an eye on dinner—their son, Jimmy, walked up to his father and said, "Dad, I want some milk."

The father went to the kitchen and got Jimmy a cup of milk. After a few minutes, Jimmy approached his father again and said, "Dad, can I watch the cartoon channel?"

"No," the father said. "We'll do that another time but not tonight."

Jimmy was not satisfied with that response. For the next few minutes, he called out, "Dad!" about every two seconds. At one point, the father turned to him and gave him a look that suggested that his son had better behave. One could see the frown on Jimmy's face that indicated he understood the message but was not pleased with it; that was when the father told me a beautiful story about Jimmy.

When he was a few months shy of his first birthday, Jimmy would stop crying only when he was in his mother's arms; he could not be consoled until his mother arrived and picked him up. This created some anxiety on the part of the father: how would he console Jimmy if the mother was busy or not around? This also made it very hard for them to get and keep babysitters. During the process of learning to speak, when Jimmy would babble, his mother would say "Mama!" while pointing at herself. Then she would point to the father and say "Dada!" Jimmy would turn to where she pointed as if he were meticulously following the instructions.

After a while, Jimmy started uttering "Ma" to his mother, but he said nothing to his father. Then he crossed a milestone from "Ma" to "Mama" but still had no word for the father. When the mother pointed to Jimmy's father and said, "Dada," Jimmy replied, "Mama!" This happened again and again.

After a long time had passed, Jimmy's father came back from work one day, and as he walked into the house, Jimmy came over with a smile on his face and, for the very first time, said, "Dada!" The father smiled, his eyes welling with tears, and lifted Jimmy into his arms.

"Yes, I am Daddy, and you are my boy," he said.

Getting a little emotional as he told me this story, he said, "That was when I felt my son had begun assimilating my role in his life as his father."

It was the true and full participation of Jimmy's father in the *natural* mother-child relationship that prompted Jimmy to begin internalizing the profound role of his father in his young life. However, it is very important to note that, despite the fact that true human fatherhood does not depend on the child's assent or expression of approval, it will still always be a great moment of joy for the father when the child begins to internalize the role of the father and, eventually, to express it verbally or nonverbally.

The very fact that human fatherhood takes a maternal form as its foundation implies that true human fatherhood is revealed and manifested only in the maternity of the woman, who embodies the womb that carries and nurtures the child who will one day utter a form of the word *Abba* to the man. In the presence of a mother (or absence, due to tragedy or neglect), human fatherhood not only takes on a maternal character (involving feeding, nurturing, comforting, attending, embracing, holding, and protecting) as the first step in the journey of fatherhood but the father also now becomes the embodiment of the *mater-persona*. In sum, a man who has engendered a child (or has adopted a child) needs a combination of two essential elements—the natural maternal character and the modeling after the divine Fatherhood of God—in order to achieve his true human fatherhood.

Similarly, the Fatherhood of God takes on a maternal character, as revealed in the scripture: "Thus the Lord says...As a mother comforts her sons so will I comfort you" (Isaiah 66:1, 13). Divine Fatherhood expresses such maternal characters as nurturing, compassion, and love. Unlike the maternal character of human fatherhood, the maternal character of God's Fatherhood already exists in God's nature. Therefore, he does not need a model to take after before he can express his maternal character. God's Fatherhood is the essence of his nature. It is the nature of God; it is not caused by a necessity outside of his being.

This participation of the man in the maternity of the woman can be built on the foundation of *true love* and *mutual self-giving*. When the child witnesses the profound action of the man *clinging* to the woman (with whom the child already has a natural relationship) with pureness of heart and truth and honesty governed by selfless love, the child will, from the core of his or her being, take a leap of faith. This childlike leap of faith is propelled by the love of the man for the mother, which prompts the child to utter the word *Father*. The man's love should be inclusive of both the child and the mother of his child because "the mother...has enormous significance in the [father-child] relationship."[48]

There are four stages in the beginning of a man's journey toward true human fatherhood:

1. The *sexual complementarity* of the man and the woman; here they give themselves to each other in a profound love while consummating their marriage.
2. The man's support of the *natural* mother-child relationship from the moment of conception to the formation of life by God in the womb of the woman and the protection and nurturing of this life by the mother.

3. The *invitation extended to the man by the mere presence of new life (birth)* to start participating in the *natural* relationship between the mother and the child.

4. The *invitation extended to the child* by the man who engendered the child to enter into a relationship with him whom the child will eventually call father.

This fourth stage will be initiated by the man through his sincere and holistic participation in the first three stages. His participation in these stages should be prompted by and conditioned upon sincere love and sacrifice and by cherishing and clinging to the mother of his child and becoming one with her.

CHAPTER FOUR

Blessed are those whose fathers "relived and reveal
on earth the very Fatherhood of God."
—*William E. May & Michael J. McGivney, quoting John Paul II*

Nothing is too much trouble for love.
—*Archbishop Desmond Tutu*

Prodigality in the Father's Love

U pon hearing the word *prodigal,* the first thing that may come to mind is sin against the virtue of prudence or the act of recklessly, immoderately, and wastefully using acquired or given resources. The word *prodigal* comes from the Latin *prodigus,* which means, "lavish,"[49] or "without restrictions, conditions, moderation, or care for the future. "Prodigality implies excess in giving but deficiency in retaining and acquiring."[50] In a moral context, prodigality is simply a lack of prudence, as illustrated by the parable of the prodigal son in the Holy Gospel of Luke (15:11–32) in which a son wastes resources and property in an extravagant manner, showing no prudence with regard to *retaining* or *acquiring*.

In this parable, the father unconditionally loves and forgives his imprudent son without judgment or condemnation; he even goes as far as lavishly celebrating the son's return. Christians believe that our Lord Jesus Christ revealed to us through this parable the essence of God as a Father who loves us bountifully with no limitation, a Father who forgives us unconditionally even before we present our faults to him, and a Father who patiently waits on us, even when we freely distance ourselves from him through human weakness or sin. Taking a second look at the parable, however, one might be tempted to question whether there is also some prodigality exhibited by the father for lavishing love and forgiveness with no restrictions or conditions, even to the extent of retaining nothing for himself; he empties his treasure of love for his son as if there were no other to love.

As Pope John Paul II points out, the father's excessive behavior illustrates the bountiful love he has for his child: "The father of the prodigal son is faithful to his fatherhood, faithful to the love that he had always lavished on his son. This fidelity is expressed in the parable not only by his immediate readiness to welcome him home when he returns after having squandered his inheritance; it is expressed even more fully by that joy, that merrymaking for the squanderer after his return, merrymaking which is so generous that it provokes hatred of the elder brother."[51] In actuality, the father's lavishing of love and forgiveness does not remove the consequences of the free choice made by the prodigal son. Rather, the father only pours out his love like a libation to create an environment of love and peace in which the son can begin from scratch to work and build himself up again through grace.

Importantly, the father of the prodigal son knows that the love he excessively and lavishly extends to his son is not his own; rather, he extends to his son what belongs to God alone but was given to the father as a gift—the essence of God. (Remember, "God is the same as his essence or nature."[52]) Therefore, this gift of love—this divine nature—cannot be acquired because *it was* and *it is*; at the same time, it cannot be retained because *it will always be*—this is the nature of God. The implication here is that, through divine grace, the father extends to the prodigal son something that is greater than his human nature and something that is inexhaustible—love.

The father does not in any way claim authorship or ownership of the love he extends to his imprudent son. He understands that this gift of love, which breeds true forgiveness, is inexhaustible; it cannot diminish or dwindle from giving or sharing, and it cannot be qualified or quantified by its nature. Hence it is meant to be spent to the fullest. The father spends this divine gift on his son with no restraints or conditions; in other words, he lavishes a love that is immune to judgment, condemnation, and moderation as well as to being governed by past transgressions. Like a libation, he pours it out to save the humanity of his son.[53] In this act of loving, he recognizes that his son is not defined by his mistakes or sins but by the goodness of his being, which was made in the image of God. "This common experience makes the prodigal son begin to see himself and his actions in their full truth (this vision in truth is a genuine form of humility); on the other hand, for this very reason he becomes a particular good for his father; the father sees so clearly the good which has been achieved thanks to a mysterious radiation of truth and love, that he seems to forget all the evil which the son had committed."[54] Therefore, the father of the prodigal son concentrates all of his spiritual energy and humanity on the contrition and broken spirit of his son; all the father can see is a contrite heart, true reconciliation, hope, and, most of all, unfathomable joy in finding what he thought had slipped away from his world.

The second aspect to note about this parable of the prodigal son is that the father lavishes God's gift not for his own benefit or self-satisfaction but for the benefit and gratification of another outside of himself, for he loves selflessly. This act of benevolence from the father ignites in the soul of the son a sense of readiness to begin his own journey of discovering God's goodness in his person. When such an act of compassion governed by true love happens, "the person who is the object of mercy does not feel humiliated, but rather found again and 'restored to value.' The father first and foremost expressed to him his joy that he has been 'found again' and that he has 'returned to life.' This joy indicates a good that has remained intact; even if he is a prodigal, a son does not cease to be truly his father's son; it also indicates a good that has been found again, which in the case of the prodigal son was his return to the truth about himself."[55] An act of mercy, forgiveness, and love that has no strings attached and is devoid of any accusations is a balm of restoration and healing and a source of internal tranquility to the one who receives it. This makes the recipients of these God-given gifts acknowledge not only the limitations of their humanity but also their inevitable dependency on God.

Human fatherhood, modeled after the supreme Fatherhood of God, should adhere to this reality that Christians hold to be true:

that humans are incapable of giving truly, sincerely, and unconditionally that act of love (which is referred to in the Holy Scripture as agape, *or selfless love) independently of God's grace.* Hence it is through this participation in the spirit of the perfect love of God that a human father is able to pour himself out like a libation for the sake of his child with no strings attached, no hidden intentions, and no anticipation of reciprocation. This selfless love generates true forgiveness, true justice, and true compassion, among other virtues. A father can only give what he has. To give true love to his child, he has to demonstrate docility and receptivity to God's love by giving himself to God; only then can he give himself to his child.

Therefore, a human father is capable of loving truly because God loved him first. God allows his love to reside in a human's soul and being and then commands the human to spend his divine love on his child. "The abundant life promised in Christ comes not from grasping but from releasing. It comes not from striving but from relinquishing. It comes not from taking as from giving."[56] In essence, the more a father extends this divine love to his child, the more the love in him increases, and the more the love in him increases, the more fulfillments he finds in his fatherhood and in his life.

Reliving the divine Fatherhood of God here on earth, the human father should govern his household and allow love to reign supreme. For that dominance and supreme reign of love to be tested, its effect has to take him to the level of *ecstasy*; this is a term St. Thomas Aquinas argued for, as an effect of love (*Summa theologica*, vol. 2, pt. I-II, q. 28, art. 3).

The word *ecstasy*, as it is predominantly used in our modern language, connotes euphoria, frenzy, and even hallucination or the state of being in a "trance," which invariably suggests a loss of human reasoning and the experience of a kind of illness or disorder. However, it is also associated with uplifting acts of selflessness engaged in for the sake of a good cause.

The word comes to us through Late Latin from the Greek *ekstasis*, which means *standing outside oneself.*[57] Simply put, in an act of ecstasy, one can go in either of two directions. One can degenerate to something that is subhuman or debased due to the effect of hallucinatory drugs or addiction.

Alternatively, one can offer oneself for the sake of love and surpass our sensible world and mere human reason to discover something that is good, sacred, virtuous, and divine in the other. The latter requires the ability to step outside of the comfort of the self and reach out to the *other* solely for good and without seeking any kind of personal benefit. So it can be said that the first act of ecstasy is simply driven by one's *selfish* love for oneself, which ends with the person, while the second act of ecstasy is simply driven by one's *selfless* love for the other and ends with the *other* while creating that internal true fulfillment for the *self*.

According to St. Thomas Aquinas, ecstasy can be the effect of something that *debases* our humanity. On the other hand it can be the effect of something that *surpasses but elevates* our humanity, as in acts of love, mercy, or forgiveness, which are all divine acts. For a human father's love for his child to reach the level of ecstasy—for him to attain the ability to live outside himself and be consumed and guided by the love for his child—love has to pass through what Archbishop Fulton Sheen (in his book *The World's First Love*) called *the seven laws of love*. I would like to draw attention to four of these laws.

THE ACT OF LOVE IS A CHOICE

A father has to freely love his child from within his soul, with neither inward nor outward coercion and without any feeling of natural or socially imposed obligation. "Every act of love is an affirmation, a preferment, a decision. But it is also a negation."[58] When a father expresses his love for his child, through either his words or his actions, that is an affirmation that he wants his child to remain in his fatherly love. The implication of this affirmation is also a negation of self-centeredness and a rejection of everything that is contrary to love or has the potential to cripple the father's ability to love unconditionally. Hence, true act of loving means doing two seemingly contradictory things at the same time to achieve the single final goal of *loving truly and unconditionally.*

"Love, is a choice, it means detachment from a previous mode of life, a breaking with old bonds…Along with detachment, there is also a deep sense of attachment to the beloved."[59] The affirmation inherent in the father's choice to love conveys an attachment, and the sincerity of his attachment simultaneously implies a detachment from everything that limits his ability to attach firmly to his love for his child.

For example, if a father has the habit of being quick-tempered and only (or mostly) communicates with his child by hurling insulting words or speaking in harsh tones and publicly embarrassing his child, this would limit healthy dialogue or meaningful discourse between them and create an environment of constant misunderstanding and tension, which is contrary to true affirmation in love: "Love is patient, love is kind…Love is not pompous, it is not inflated, it is not rude, it does not seek its own interests, it is not quick-tempered…It…endures all things" (1 Corinthians 13:4–7). Since such habits hinder true affirmation in love, the father has to be willing and determined to negate any unhealthy habit that makes it impossible for him to truly affirm his love for his child.

In this context, the human father must engage in some honest reflection. What, he must ask, are the things in his life that hinder him from attaching to his beloved child? These can include such things as his personality; his habits or addictions; his inhumane attitude toward the mother of his child; his inappropriate expressions of anger or frustration; his lack of attention and concern; his lack of dedication to teaching his child basic human, moral, and religious values; his dishonesty; and his verbal or physical abuse of his child or the mother of his child. So if a father chooses to attach himself to his child based on what he assumes is love, and he is still unable to detach himself from these other things that make that attachment unrealistic or even impossible, then he not only comes across to his child as being a dishonest father but is also dishonest to himself. Moreover, that child will eventually be robbed of his right to a father's true love.

CHOOSING TO LOVE RESULTS IN IDENTIFICATION WITH THE BELOVED

Every father sincerely choosing to love must be ready to embrace the sacrifice that comes with this choice. One essential aspect of this sacrifice is *surrender*, which the father must do only for the sake of love and not for anything contrary, for "surrendering to anything other than love would be idiocy."[60] Sometimes a father has to surrender his own will so that the will of the child can take precedence. "Once the will makes the choice [to love], surrender follows, for freedom is ours only to give away. 'My will is mine to make it thine,' is on the lips of every lover."[61] By surrendering, the father who loves is one step closer to identifying with his beloved child.

It was this same unconditional love that prompted God the Son, in accordance with the will of God the Father, to surrender his divine throne in heaven (without brandishing his equality with the Father), come into the human world, and become like us. God surrendered himself and died for love in order to lift us up again and allow us to enjoy the freedom of loving God and one another. Simply put, in love, God identified himself with us and became like us, his beloved, so that we could in turn become like him, the lover.[62]

Therefore, *identification* is a vital element in the father-child relationship. "Love is said to transform the lover into the loved because by love the lover is moved towards the thing loved."[63] The father, through his love, identifies with the beloved, his child, who consciously or unconsciously assimilates the movement of fatherly love, and this assimilated love within the child prompts the child to obey the father. Hence, the father receives from his child a true obedience prompted by pure love instead of obedience prompted by coercion, force, or fear of disciplinary consequence.

In every true love of a father for his child should exist the reality of surrendering his own personal needs—his self-satisfaction, his time, his individual pleasures, and his own well-being—for the sake of *identifying* with the needs and the well-being of his child. This gracious act of the father will become then, an *invitation* to that child to freely enter into a loving relationship with him. This loving relationship is devoid of any kind of obligation; rather, it is propelled by a freedom borne out by the child's gratitude and appreciation for the unconditional love and altruism on the part of the child's father. The result of these acts of *identification* and *invitation* on the part of the father, and of the child's acceptance of his invitation, is a total *oneness between father and child.*

LOVE REQUIRES A CONSTANT DE-EGOTIZATION

When choosing to love, thoughts of *I* and *me* should start yielding to thoughts of *we* and *us.* This implies that a father who has chosen to love his child has to stop thinking in singularity and start thinking in duality, in plurality, and even in multiplicity. "Ego cuts us off from other people, from

Nature, from God, from our authentic self, from our true responsibility, and from fulfilling our destiny. Our ego is the great usurper...The ego convinces us that we are truly separate beings with ultimately a separate will, having no inherent connection with other people or with God."[64] When love is concentrated on *oneself*, it becomes dormant and heads to annihilation. *De-egotization* occurs when a father understands that the *self* (his fatherhood) has meaning only in relation to the *other* (the child). "The needs of [the child] may become so imperative that [the father] may have to sacrifice [his] own comfort for [his child]. Love that does not expand dies of its own too-much."[65] The more we spend our love on others, the more we begin to live outside of ourselves and give meaning to our own human existence.

De-egotization begins when a father sees his love for his child not as something that is invented by him, comes from him, or belongs to him but as something that was given to him by God and meant to be returned back to God through the extension of that love to his child. In other words, human fatherhood should be like an open vessel, which God uses to distribute his divine love to his children. For this reason, no human father has the right to claim ownership of the love that properly belongs to God by, for example, restricting, retaining, placing conditions on, or apportioning it. "And so whenever you are loving, you are sharing in divinity and grace."[66]

In addition, *de-egotization* begins when a father goes outside himself and, instead of concentrating on his own goodness, begins to concentrate on the goodness in his child's being. Therefore, the father has to learn to separate the child's being from the child's actions. An inappropriate action taken by the child is not the whole definition of the being of that child, "for there are oceans of goodness within the human being."[67] When a father spends all his time constantly seeing the mistakes, weaknesses, or wrongs committed by his child, he not only neglects the goodness in the humanity of the child but also implies that he considers himself infallible. Therefore, to avoid this unhealthy self-centeredness, the father has to understand that the love he gives to his child does not belong to him; it is given to him to be spent outside of himself and to be spent to the fullest.

THE END OF ALL HUMAN LOVE IS DOING THE WILL OF GOD

Every human act that has a beginning inevitably has a destined end, and once we come to clearly understand that destined end, it helps us guide or define the means; that is, the end becomes a justification of the means. When a father truly perceives that the single intended purpose of his love for his child is to do the will of God and accomplish what is pleasing to God, that becomes his motivation for adopting a better means to reach this single purpose. "Love has no other destiny than to obey Christ...Hence, all perfect love must end on the note: 'Not my will but Thine be done, O Lord!'"[68] The father in the parable of the prodigal son has one intention, and he allows his love for his son to guide him to the act of forgiveness, which is divine and pleasing to God.

So when a father, in the expression of what he presumes to be love, acts contrary to the will of God (who is the source of love), he is not only doing injustice to the divine gift of love but also separating himself from the source of his love, God the Father. "Creation declares that humans are born of love and for love, created in the image of God who is Love. Love is our source and love is to be our fulfillment."[69] A father is prone to doing the will of God in an act of love for his child when he allows himself to be consumed and absorbed in love rather than obsessed with it. When a father allows himself to be consumed and absorbed in love, he abandons himself to be guided by love, but when he becomes obsessed with love, he pretends to guide love, which leads to depravity. The truth is that no human has the capability or power to guide love, rather, the nature of love, is to guide the human person.

The consequence of a human father being obsessed with and pretending to guide love is that he will gradually drift away from the act of giving love and turn to controlling and possessing it; he might even go to the extreme of subjecting the gift of love to his own desire in order to brandish his persona and power, which leads him in the opposite direction—away from the will of God, who is love. Whenever a father expresses love to his child, he should ask himself whether an act of love will result in doing the will of God and whether what he is doing is pleasing and glorifying to God.

CHAPTER FIVE

Presence is a mode of being available or open in a situation with the wholeness of one's unique, individual being, a gift of the self which can only be given freely, invoked or evoked.
—*J. G. Paterson and L. T. Zderad*

The Act of True Presence in Human Fatherhood

After the creation of the universe and humanity by God, why does God continue to linger in human history (as the Holy Scripture reveals) instead of abandoning the universe to the human race? Why did he choose to maintain his presence? Was leaving his creation to itself a difficult thing for him to do? Alternatively, did he remain present because *he is a being whose nature it is to remain immanent in his creations,* even when they are mere mortal and passing beings? This very perplexing question is what seems to have prompted this psalmist's question in the Holy Scripture: "O Lord, our Lord...what are humans that you are mindful of them, mere mortals that you care for them?" (Psalm 8:2, 5). The psalmist could not totally grasp the mind and intelligence of a God who lavishes his infinite divine presence on mere finite being.

There must be an efficacy in a true act of presence that explains why God has, from the beginning, continued to reveal his presence in human history. It is even more evident in our human experience. We always want to be present for those who really love us, encourage us, share our feelings, and remain honest with us. We feel different when they have been absent from us for very long periods of time; we feel as if something inside of us is missing, we feel a part of ourselves is apart from us. William Shakespeare alludes to this human emotional reality in *The Two Gentlemen of Verona* (Act III, Scene I.), when Valentine expresses a feeling of *self from self* as the Duke banishes him from his daughter, Silvia, whom Valentine is in love with.

In contrast, the moment we see our loved ones, we feel whole again; we run to them and hold them and want simply to remain in their arms and say nothing, as if we were inhaling and consuming their presence. During these moments, we hardly pause to ask why we feel this way. Rather, we permit ourselves to be consumed in the moment and in the power of presence.

The process entails an unconscious and profound exchange of giving and receiving of self, which can happen only in what Martin Buber calls the *Ich und Du* relationship, or the *I and Thou* relationship, which exists when there is a complete, spiritual, and mutual giving and receiving of self.

To understand the efficacy and power of the word *presence* when used in reference to father-child relationships, let us go back to its meaning. According to the *Oxford American Dictionary*, the word *presence* refers to "the state or fact of existing, occurring, or being in a place or in a thing."

I was a young boy when my father passed away. At the time, I was inconsolable. I had lost not only my father but also my inspiration, and I didn't know what would become of my family. I had five younger siblings, and thinking of my mother taking care of us all by herself was too difficult for me to bear. It was at this moment that my maternal uncle, Father Damian, stepped into our lives. He sat me and my siblings down, looked into our eyes, and said, "From now on, I will be the father you will all know; I will have you all under my wings from today until the end; I will stand in for your late father and be there to support your mother."

This brought great consolation to us. From then on, my uncle was *present* for us. We saw him every day; even when we were far away at school, we always heard from him. After a while, we gradually internalized his presence, and it brought us great tranquility and hope; in time, it alleviated the sadness of losing our father. In place of despair, it gave us hope; because he wanted us to do well in life, we were motivated to want the same and to be able to contribute to society. His true presence with us made us feel that we had a great friend who loved us and whose advice could shape our inner characters; he instilled in us the confidence we needed to face life's challenges. Even when we are far away from home, his presence remains in our lives as we try to live out the values he instilled in us. In other words, my uncle not only remained externally present with us in place and time but internally present as well.

Paterson and Zderad define *presence* as "a mode of being available or open in a situation with the wholeness of one's unique, individual being; a gift of the self which can only be given freely, invoked or evoked."[70] This definition might be said to take as its foundation Martin Buber's *Ich und Du* (*I and -Thou*) and *Ich und Es* (*I and It*) modes of human relationships. The *I-It* relationship is a relationship between an *I* (a person) and an *It* (a thing), while the *I-Thou* relationship is a relation-ship between an *I* (a person) and a *Thou* (another). However, in the *I-Thou* relationship, the individuality of the *I* is not compro-mised; rather, for the *I* to affirm a true and authentic presence, it is necessary that he or she is cognizant of the *Thou*. This is a profound relationship entailing a mutual exchange of the self, a dialogue of mind and heart, and a oneness of being (a unity from duality).

In this relationship, the *I* and the *Thou* relate to each other as subjects of the same nature rather than as objects. For Buber, this type of relationship is what defines and gives meaning to our human existence.[71] We might say both subjects are able to participate wholly in each other's person. This interpersonal relationship (*actual presence*) can be seen in God the Father's relationship with all his creatures. From the beginning of humanity, according to sacred scripture, this idea of *actual presence* has been evident in the relationship between the supreme Fatherhood of God and us, his children, for he has always demonstrated his presence in our human lives and in our relationships with him in spiritual, physical, and mystical ways.

However, a fundamental question remains: why did God perceive his divine presence as being essential to humanity? The answer is that *God, by his divine nature, is love, and this love, by its nature and characteristics, is ordained to expand and to be extended to the other.* Love can only correspond to its nature and become meaningful and fruitful when it extends to the other in true communion, and the only prerequisite for true communion is an *actual presence*. For this reason, God, whose nature is love, divinely exists to remain eternally present in human history; this way we can participate fully in communion with his love.

The nature of human fatherhood is the effect of divine love; it came into existence through love for the sake of extending God's love to children. In order for this to occur, each father has to allow his presence to reign in his relationship with his child, and an *I-Thou* relationship must develop whereby the father gives himself to his child in fullness; the child must then, in turn, receive him and, in reciprocation, give himself or herself to the father, who, again, in turn, must receive his child in fullness.

Divine love, through which we were all created, cannot be extended in solitude but only through the *I-Thou* relationship that is possible through *actual presence*, because in this relationship there is a mutual exchange of self. "It is a Gospel truth concerning the gift of self, without which the person cannot 'fully find himself.'"[72] God first gave himself to us in wholeness so that we could in return give our whole selves to him and to one another. Only in this mode of relationship between the *I* and the *Thou,* through the *Eternal Thou* (this is how Martin Buber refers to God), is human life made meaningful and consummated.

True presence in a father-child relationship is not merely a visible or physical presence or a father's participation in the life of a child when the need arises. Rather, true presence entails a profound and whole mutual exchange of self, an unspoken dialogue of hearts and minds, a sharing of intimate thoughts in a spiritual unity of beings, a full awareness of the other, and a beholding of the other in the wholeness of being, not as an object but as a subject. Therefore, the true presence of a father in the life of his child does not merely entail a physical presence but also an *internal* presence that positively transfigures the child from within. In such a relationship, true presence should not be conditional, circumstantial, or even compulsive; rather, it should flow freely from the father's innermost nature.

For example, I once met a friend of mine and her father, and I teasingly said to the father in front of the daughter, "Is she behaving well?"

"Yes, she is the best," the father said without hesitation.

As he said that, the daughter reached for her father and gave him a lovely hug. With a smile of gratitude, she said, "I love you, Dad."

The father gave her a warm cuddle and said to her, "I will always love you."

In that exchange, I could see that a true and profound feeling of love existed between the father and the daughter. In admiration, I said, "How wonderful and happy every child's life in this world would be if every father could feel the same way about his children as you do about your daughter; further, how fulfilling fatherhood would be for every father if every child could feel the way your daughter feels about you. I know that is not always the case."

Further listening to the father, I could perceive that his relationship with his daughter was based on openness and acceptance and speaking to each other's hearts and being honest with each other. Sometimes that honesty could mean prudent rebukes, appropriate reprimands, or the enacting of discipline to stir the child in the right direction in her life.

"She is my daughter," he said. "God gave her to me as a gift. But I freely chose what was given to me."

Reflecting on this last statement of this, the phrase that came to mind was *true communion*. The further I thought about what the central element in the act of true presence in a father-child relationship is, the clearer it was to me that *a father cannot be truly present with his child where there is no true communion*. In the above encounter, the father took the initiative, chose his daughter, opened his heart (the seat of true communion), and let her in. In reciprocation, the daughter opened her own heart and let her father in. Only in this reality of *true communion* can *true presence* flourish, as revealed in the Holy Scripture. In order for God to be truly present with his people, first he chose to enter into a communion with his chosen ones: "But this is the covenant which I will make with the house of Israel after those days, says the Lord. I will place my law within them, and write it upon their hearts; I will be their God, and they shall be my people" (Jeremiah 31:31). It was in this communion that God remained truly present with them and revealed himself to them. The first step a human father must take to enter into a *true communion* with his child is to choose the *person* of his child as a sacred gift from God and open his heart to let in his child.

Even if a father provides for his child, pays for his child's education, and takes responsibility for the health and well-being of his child, that does not necessarily translate to true presence. Granted, the mentioned elements (paying for education, responsibility for the health and moral well being of a child) are indisputable aspects of being present in a child's life, however, in order to be truly present, the father must, in the end, enter into a *true communion* with his child in which there is an exchange of hearts.

This *true presence of a father in the life of a child* could be misconstrued as an abstract concept, but, in actuality, it is simply the result of the natural evolution of the father-child relationship. When a child begins to internalize what he or she perceives in the person of the father and, from this perception, forms his or her own person, the image and likeness of the father begins to take root in the child. This is what it means for a father to be a model for his child. Even in the inevitable absence of the physical father—whether permanent (due to death) or brief (if, for example, he is deployed to serve in the military)—that image of the father becomes for the child an unwritten and invisible guide to a positive attitude about life and to the absolute ideal and supreme Fatherhood of God; this is especially true for a child who is fortunate enough to experience at a mature age the person of his or her father. The continual presence of the earthly father becomes a beacon to encountering the heavenly Father from whom all human fatherhood emanates.

As God the Father established his presence *with us* and *in us*, forming us in his image and letting his spirit and grace dwell within us, he became a practical source of the spiritual strength, encouragement, faith, and inspiration from which we fashion our own practical human and spiritual lives. In the same fashion, the image of a human father should become to his child a source of inspiration, courage, aspiration, determination, true love, true freedom, respect, and regard for others. Inspired thus, the child gradually forms his or her own human image, which takes its form through the presence of an earthly father, which emanates from

God the Father. The human father's act of living now becomes the bedrock for his child upon which he or she may build a spiritual, mental, emotional, psychological, and social foundation.

As a child growing up, I experienced the greatest love a father could give to his child. In every situation, my siblings and I remained my father's priority, even to the detriment of his own personal comfort. I remember watching my father and mother sitting down and discussing our education, well-being, health care, and day-to-day activities. In the person of my father, I witnessed the greatest love a man could have for his wife. In fact, my mother has never stopped talking about how much her husband loved her.

Through these experiences, I learned the virtue and efficacy of true love: it endures all times and seasons, it is always engraved in our hearts, and it defies all human odds. My life philosophy is that it is better to try and fail than to not try at all. I picked this up from my father. He would always tell us that the possibility of failing is not a reason to not try to achieve something virtuous. He always reminded us that true and lasting success in life does not come on a silver platter but instead arises by the sweat of our brows, and that is what makes it worthwhile.

When my parents took us shopping for clothing, we would first buy clothes for sports and school, and then we would buy special clothes for church. I was often tempted to wear the church clothing for other activities because it looked nicer in quality and style, but my father would always tell me it was for church only. When I asked him why my church clothes were so much nicer than my everyday clothes, my father said, "Because they are for God, and God always deserves something special." That very concept—that God was special and deserved our best—was pounded into our minds and souls to the extent that it remained within me even in my imperfection. Despite the absence of my father, I can still feel the impact of what he instilled in me; I can still hear his voice echoing within my heart as a guide in my present life.

All in all, my father remained actually (externally and internally) present then, both to my siblings and me, even when death made his physical presence impossible. He remains internally present and influences us in our personal lives, and for that we are grateful. Sadly, there are many children who lost their fathers at younger ages, and they may not be as fortunate to have had the same experience with their biological fathers as I did, and that is why it is very important for the extended family members, the community, and religious organizations to ensure that these children have true father figures who always remain truly present and guide them through a healthy father-child relationship.

The Act of True Presence in Human Fatherhood

Among the kinds of fathers who can be physically *present with* their children but not actually *present in* their lives are abusive fathers, fathers who do not treat their children with compassion and believe they should punish rather than administer appropriate disciplines and reprimands to teach and place their children on the right paths in their lives, fathers who see the mistakes of their children as irreversible failures instead of as ways to lead them to true knowledge, and fathers who refuse to acknowledge that their children will change over time if patiently and properly led.

A father-child relationship with a great deal of *presence with* (physical presence) but without *presence in* (internal presence) can easily lead the father to neglect the child and deprive him or her of positive human qualities. This is the major reason why some fathers can easily walk out on their own children in situations of a separation or a divorce, with no regret or remorse. Right from the onset, there is the absence of that internal and spiritual connection or communion that is necessary for a healthy father-child relationship. Invariably, such fathers neglect the existential fact that by bringing a new life into the world, whether or not it was planned, they automatically incurred a bilateral covenant with the Giver of Life (God). The concrete object of this bilateral covenant between a human father and the divine is *new life,* and the pact of this covenant is an unconditional *actual presence* on the part of the father in relation to his child; therefore, the only thing necessary for this bilateral covenant to come into existence is the gift of *new life.*

When a man and woman enter into a sexual relationship with the potential for creating new life, they are freely expressing their readiness to enter into this bilateral covenant with God. In other words, a man and a woman saying yes to each other in a sexual relationship and therefore being open to life is an invitation to God to begin molding and fashioning this new life in the womb of the woman; with the assurance on the part of the couple that they will always remain physically and internally present while nurturing this life. Hence human fatherhood is constituted not only by the *presence with a child* but also the *presence in a child,* as an imitation of the divine Fatherhood of God, who made us in his image *(his presence in us)* and his love by infusing in us his Holy Spirit; by his *presence with us* and his *presence in us,* the divine Father through Christ becomes our source of inspiration, life, hope, truth, and practical holiness.

CHAPTER SIX

He didn't tell me how to live; he lived and let me watch him do it.
—Clarence Budington Kelland.

The great leader is seen as servant first.
—Robert K. Greenleaf

The Father's True Leadership Through Acts of True Service

T he word *leader* is commonly associated with power and authority. Too often, a leader is defined as one through whom all decisions must pass before they are implemented and one whose will everyone else must be subjected to; a leader is also frequently perceived as one to whom all accounts are rendered. Sometimes a leader is misconceived as a tyrant, dictator, or micromanager or as a kind of demiurge whose self-centeredness takes precedence.

This distorted conception of leadership takes us back to the beginning of the Holy Scripture—namely, to the episode of the original sin of pride in the Genesis account of divine creation, in which humanity distorted God's commandment of steward-ship, which went as follows: "Fill the earth and subdue it. Have dominion over…all the living things that move on earth" (1:28). Humanity misinterpreted this, as meaning that it could use its freedom and authority to bend every created thing to the ser-vice of its own needs, comforts, and pleasures—an interpreta-tion that absolutely contradicts the true act of stewardship.

"It is said that human beings are called to rule in the sense of holding an ascendancy over the whole of visible creation, in the manner of a king."[73] The consequence of the distorted understanding of this divine commandment is revealed in our present-day misconception of the word *leadership.* Christians believe that God intended for humanity to be commissioned as a *steward* of creation by which it could manifest and extend its leadership, its kingship for the sole purpose of extending the love and glory of God on earth. "The inner meaning of this kingship is, as Jesus reminds his disciples, one of service."[74]

This brings us to the difference between the *act of human ser-vice through human leadership* (serving by one's leadership) and the *act of human leadership through human service* (leading by one's service) in a father-child relationship. In the former, *leadership* precedes *service*; while in the latter, *service* precedes *leadership* and corresponds with divine intention as revealed by Christ. Therefore, *service* should precede and be the cause of *leadership*. An act of leadership that flows from an act of true service is in conformity with Christian values and Christian charity.

Our Lord Jesus Christ reminded his disciples of the divine truth that the *human person is called to the vocation of servant-hood* when he said, "Whoever wishes to be first among you shall be your servant..."[75] This implies that the prerequisite for being a good and true leader as a father is to act in the name of true service. Robert Greenleaf, who founded the Modern Servant Leadership Movement and coined the term *Servant Leadership* (leading by one's service), affirms the notion that "the servant-leader...is servant first...It begins with the natural feeling that one wants to serve..."[76] He says elsewhere, "Leadership was bestowed upon a man who was by nature a servant. It was something given, or assumed, that could be taken away. His servant nature was the real man, not bestowed, not assumed, and not to be taken away. He was servant first."[77] In essence, God made us so that we could serve one another, and it is through our acts of service and stewardship that we demonstrate true greatness.

In *service through leadership*, the *I* is always the focus. It is all going to be about my authority, my position, my power, my reputation, my decisions, and my plans to crown my leadership with success, even if it means going against universal moral values or laws. The single objective here is the success of the *I*. This type of self-centered mind-set breeds exploitation, tyranny, competition, and sometimes viciousness.

By contrast, in *leadership through service,* the *Thou* (the *other*) is the focus and priority; the one being served is the center of attention instead of the one serving. There is no competition or grabbing onto power or authority; rather, there is a pure spirit of charity. Therefore, the *I* should constantly ask what he or she can do to make the *Thou* feel loved and cared for as well as what he or she can do to promote the dignity and the rights of the other without anticipating—whether obviously or surreptitiously—gain or reward. In the mind of God as revealed by Christ, "Greatness consisted not in reducing others to one's service, but in reducing oneself to their service. The test was not what service can I extract, but what service can I give."[78] A father, striving to serve (to lead by his service) first, which is simply *craving to go out of himself and reach out to his child,* becomes an extension of the love of God to that child, thereby actively living out the true purpose of his humanity.

We were created for this reason; we were made through pure love in order to extend that same pure love. Our Lord Jesus Christ proclaimed, "The Son of Man did not come to be served but to serve and to give his life as a ransom" (Matthew 20:28).

Through this *service* of Christ, his glory, divine authority, and power were manifested in such a way that his disciples were prompted to call him *Lord*. Christ speaking in such a fashion as to bring to the forefront the act of *service* and to proclaim it a prerequisite to greatness and true leadership is an indication that true stewardship is strongly connected to our nature.

When it comes to father-child relationships, a father who wishes to become a *true leader* in the eyes of his children must first be a *true servant*. As a true steward of sacred life (that of his child), he must ensure that his child perceives him first as a servant and true steward who is living his life with a sense that he will one day *render an account of his stewardship to God*.

In order for a human father to begin creating this perception of a true leader in his children, he must be willing to embrace the following.

THE TRUE MEANING OF HIS HUMANITY

In the midst of our changing world, the father has to confront his own existence in reference to his creation and answer for himself these fundamental questions:

- Why was it so important that God created me?
- What is the meaning and purpose of my existence?

- As a father, how do I treat my child and how does this compare to the type of father I am called to be?

These profound questions could be answered precisely in the spirit of Saint Francis of Assisi:

Lord, you made me to be a servant of your love and goodness, an extension of your essence.

Where there is hatred in the life of my child, as a father you made me to be a servant of love.

Where there is despair in the life of my child, as a father you made me to be a servant of hope.

Where there is darkness and sadness in the life of my child, you made me as a father to be a servant of light and joy.

Where there is doubt in the life of my child, you made me as a father to be a servant of faith and enlightenment.

O divine Master, you made me as a father to seek to serve my child, instead of seeking to be served.

You made me as a father to seek to love my child instead of seeking to be loved.

You made me as a father to understand my child instead of seeking to be understood.

You made me as a father to be a servant of your gift of divine forgiveness to my child unconditionally when there is error, so that I may receive more of your divine mercy.

Oh, Father, you made me an earthly father so that I may lay down my own life for your new gift of life in my child.

So, at the end of my own earthly and temporal life of father-hood, I would be truly transformed into that life that is destined for eternity and finds its consummation in the spirit of supreme Fatherhood of God through Christ Jesus.

When a father is a true steward of sacred life, serving God in his child, not only does his fatherhood become a means of his own salvation but also his life on earth becomes a fulfillment of the intention of God the Father, and that makes his life as a father on earth worth living.

GIVING DUE AND UNDIVIDED ATTENTION TO HIS STEWARDSHIP OF SACRED LIFE

One of the greatest attributes of a true servant or steward is his or her ability to give undivided attention to the good causes he or she serves. Sometimes the servant's attention intensifies to such an extent—he or she becomes so alert and so focused—that by merely nodding the head or making eye contact the servant is able to interpret the intentions, feelings, and needs of those being served. This gesture of humility on the part of the ser-vant generates feelings of gratitude, trust, and understanding in the person being served. According to French Philosopher Simone Weil, "In the intellectual order, the virtue of humility is nothing more nor less than the power of attention."[79] The act of true humility is the awareness or the acknowledgment of the other's presence with its potentials—that is the simple definition of positive attention. In other words, when one gives one's undivided attention to someone or something, one affirms one's recognition of that person or thing. One has then gone out of oneself to recognize the presence of the other and see what the other needs for fulfillment and what the other can offer and contribute to make a positive difference in the world.

Invariably, true attention entails charitably shifting one's focus to acknowledge the humanity of other people. When a justifiable attention is given to every spectrum of the human race, irrespective of background, race, culture, geographical location, or belief, it effectively communicates human equality, dignity, and respect, affirming the presence of others and recognizing their uniqueness in a common human family. In Simone Weil's words, "Equality is the public recognition…of the principle, that an equal degree of attention is due to the needs of all human beings."[80] Simply put, going out of one's way to give one's undivided attention to the other is a prerequisite for true servant-hood, true love, and a true spirit of acceptance of our communal humanity in the midst of our diversity.

Some fathers pay insufficient or scarce attention to their relationships with their children. Without being conscious of it, they relate to their children as if they do not really matter. These fathers put their entire focus on whether their children listen to them, whether their commands and demands are adhered to, and whether their personal terms are being met. Hardly do they take the time to listen attentively to the voices of their own children, hear their frustrations and concerns, feel their pains and joys, and participate fully in their lives with undivided attention. When a father embraces his servitude to the cause that transcends this mundane world, he will begin to carry this new sacred life of his child like an earthenware jar that demands his ultimate attention, for it is delicate and fragile.

In my previous pastoral assignment at Good Shepherd Catholic Church, we were blessed to have a grade school (preschool through eighth grade). There was nothing more fulfilling for me than visiting these young students, reading to them, answering their questions, and spending quality time with them. Their pure joy and happiness was infectious, a great source of rejuvenation. The youngest of the students (the three-year-olds) were called the *Little Angels* — and that is what they were. I always looked forward to visiting them. As soon as I stepped into their classrooms, they dropped everything, ran toward me, crowding around me, speaking all at the same time, calling my name. They were excited to show me their new shoes or clothes; share what they did over the weekend (sometimes without being aware they were spilling some family secrets) or to tell upcoming plans. I was always invited to come and see their individual class projects.

In the midst of this delightful whirlwind, I made an effort to give each child an equal (qualitative) and justifiable amount of attention. I walked to each of their desks and squeezed into their seats (which were the smallest you can imagine). I answered their questions and listened to them actively. I nodded my head in affirmation, gasped in astonishment, dropped my jaw, or lifted my eyebrows in surprise. I examined their projects and congratulated each one of them for doing a fantastic job, even if they had just drawn lines all over a plain sheet of white paper—these were the greatest projects imaginable as far as they and I were concerned. I felt tremendously fulfilled by how the attention I gave them caused purity of joy and excitement visible on their faces. Some of the children even jumped up and down, ran to their friends, and told them how great I said their projects were. They were always joyful and excited every time I walked into their classrooms, not because I brought them candy, toys, or gifts, but because they knew I was genuinely interested in their well-being. They knew that they mattered to me and that they were guaranteed to get a bit of my time and attention. I tried to make each child feel important because each one of them was important—and no one should take that divine gift away from them.

Most child psychologists would agree that making a child feel important is central to building up his or her self-esteem as healthy and strong, and it will eventually help the child believe in his or her potentials and abilities and actualize them for the good of all humankind.

By virtue of a father's true stewardship, he is obliged to give his undivided attention to his child. In a healthy human relationship, a wholesome attention is one of the greatest gifts we can offer to the other. When this gift of attention is given in wholeness to children, fathers not only begin to affirm and reaffirm the humanity of their children—their presence, talents, and divine images—but also they begin to wholly participate in their lives. They begin to share their children's joy and sorrow, disappointment and gratitude, and confusion and longing for knowledge, as well as their successes and setbacks and their hurts and healings. Without judging or condemning them, fathers begin to serve God by guiding their children from where they are to where they are destined to be. Only through this type of interpersonal relationship can fathers begin to build understanding and trust in their relationships with their children and embody in love their stewardship as they lead their children to lives that are worth living.

When I mention that a father should give undivided attention to his child, I do not mean just any kind of attention; rather, I mean *positive attention*, an attention focused on perfecting the personhood of the child. Appropriate reprimands and praises should affirm the child as a person, which will enable the child to positively assert his or her existence on the world stage. By doing this, the father takes the midwifery role of assisting his child in giving birth to the God-given talent, ingenuity, and goodness that are already gestating in the child's being. Beholding his child always in a positive light, the father can spot the child's talent and goodness, and begins to tell the child what he sees. This enables his child to start internalizing and identifying with the goodness, talents, and gifts that he or she has been divinely given, which will hopefully lead him or her to share these with others. This service on the part of the father gives the child the necessary tools to actualize his or her full potential. In essence, the father, by his act of service, leads his child from the world of potentiality to the world of actuality. In contrast to *negative attention* (focusing squarely on the mistakes and "flaws" of a child), which diminishes the personhood of the child while opening the door to a debased self-esteem, *positive attention* dignifies the personhood of the child, and the father must understand this.

Blessed is the father who exercises prudence in his undivided attention to more than one child. This father should equally (qualitatively) share his attention among his children to avoid unnecessary competition or feelings of neglect. For example, when a father walks in the door and the youngest child runs into his arms to greet him, his next act should be (while still holding and lavishing his attention on the youngest child) to walk over to the older child, put his hands on the child's shoulder, and ask, "How are you doing today? How did your day go?" (Of course, he should also extend the same attention to his wife.) In this manner, the father teaches all his children a valuable lesson about the spirit of sharing. The children—both the younger and the older one—would learn to share their father's love and avoid competing for his attention.

Once a father, through his actions, unintentionally or intentionally displays favoritism for, gives more attention to, or loves one child over another, his true stewardship will be compromised. He will, by this divisive action, cause a conflict among his children. Sometimes this *parentally caused conflict* may linger in the lives of children even into their adulthood. This is a common reality in some families today. One truth a father should be conscious of is that every new sacred life, born or unborn, is endowed with divine goodness, talents, gifts, and ingenuities that are unique to each person but were ordained to be shared with others. Like a midwife, the father should attentively serve his children equally by helping each one fully realize his or her innate goodness, talents, and gifts.

COMMUNICATING IN WORDS THAT EXPRESS AND REVEAL HIS STEWARDSHIP

Sometimes we underestimate the profound power and effects that our words have on our children. One word can unlock places in the heart of a child that a combination of physical strength, intimidation, power, force, and fear could never unlock. Words can give tremendous hope, wipe away tears of sorrow, breed love, heal a wounded heart, and bring lasting peace and harmony. They can also, however, cause unimaginable ruin, build fences of discrimination and separation, bring about despair and disharmony, and unintentionally cause unimaginable damage to a father-child relationship. Therefore, a father should be mindful of his use of words so that they may provide insight, human wisdom and spiritual nourishment to the soul of his child.

One day, I visited with my former archbishop—the Most Reverend Charles J. Chaput—and made a request of him. After some reflection, he prudently said, "Father Faustinus, at the moment I cannot grant your request."

I was disappointed and inquired why he could not. While explaining his reasons, which were honest and genuine, he made a statement that changed the entire trajectory of my mood and swung me from disappointment to understanding and gratitude. After explaining his first reason, he said, "Also, I share a responsibility and accountability for your life as a person, and I share a responsibility for your priesthood and vocation. I care about you as a father."

At these words, my disappointment and frustration evaporated. Instead of nursing my disappointment over his rejection of my request, I found myself reflecting on his fatherly care, goodwill, and understanding. He did not say, "Because I am the archbishop." Rather, he spoke to me from the perspective of a steward and spiritual shepherd who understood his vocation as a servant of my human life first, my spiritual life second, and my vocation third. By causing me to have this perception, he fruitfully led me to the light of awareness and understanding in a way that was informative and healing. His leadership was made manifest, for he led me from where I was to where I should be. That was a lesson for life that showed how true leadership can exist through an act of true service.

I believe that my informative encounter with the archbishop may serve as a model of communication in father-child relationships. A father should be able to give a plausible and convincing reason to his child as to why he is demanding a particular action or why he thinks his idea would serve his child better than what the child is requesting. A father should be able to explain to his child why he is encouraging him or her to carry out a particular action or refrain from it and why he is demanding the child's obedience in a particular circumstance. Unfortunately, some fathers don't always speak with such patience and wisdom. Too often, when speaking to their children, they do not use their words wisely. They may, for example, say any of the following:

- "Because I said so!"
- "Because I'm your father! That's why!"
- "Because I pay the bills in this house!"
- "Because I am in charge here!"
- "Because this is my house, and if you want to stay here, you have to obey my rules!"

These kinds of phrases offer no plausible, informative reasons for the father's decisions, and they do not bring solutions to any problems; rather, they express self-centeredness. When a father uses these kinds of words, he communicates not his true stewardship but (intentionally or unintentionally) *his arrogance and his selfishness,* which "destroys the meaning of life; it destroys the meaning of love; it reduces the human person to a subhuman level."[81] This self-centeredness now takes precedence over love, meaningful dialogue, patience, and understanding. These kinds of words communicate that one is losing that pure moral authority governed by the kind of love that emanates from within. A father's constant reference to his own authority, title, and power—as if they were the sum definition of his person—expose an ugly obsession with control and dictatorship. At this point, the father's stewardship is debased because he is serving himself and not his child—the cause that (should have) prompted his fatherhood.

A father who truly understands his fatherhood as emanating from the Fatherhood of God should begin choosing words that not only reflect his servant-hood and true values but also express his stewardship to a sacred life and to his divine vocation as a father. For example, a father might instead say the following to his child:

- "Because I care for your life and well-being."
- "Because I am the servant of your life, and I am responsible for you."

- "Because I am going to account for you before God and human."
- "Because I want you to be internally happy."
- "Because I will feel sad to see you hurt."
- "Because your presence means a lot to my life."
- "Because I want to see you use your freedom wisely and in a way that will bring joy to you."
- "Because I want you to be internally fulfilled and make a difference in your life and the lives of others."

Using these kinds of phrases, a father affirms his full presence in the life of his child and brings meaning to his stewardship, which now becomes *internally engraved* in his child. To the child, the name of his or her father becomes synonymous with the one who is always there in good times and in bad times or the one who laid down his life in sacrifice so that the son or daughter could become somebody. The child now sees the father as the one whose shoulder is always there to cry on when the world is too much to bear and the one who always has that fatherly touch that says it will be OK and it is going to get better.

In a father-child relationship, the father who strives to become a true *servant first* has made a choice to live his life for his child, and in doing so, he lays down the solid foundation of pure and true leadership. The father who strives to become a *leader first* has made a choice to live his life for himself and himself alone, making a jump away from his vocation (servant-hood, or giving himself as a gift to others) and his final destiny. "It is through the free gift of self that one truly finds oneself... As a person, he can give himself to another person or to other persons, and ultimately to God, who is the author of our being and who alone can fully accept our gift. Man is alienated if he refuses to transcend himself and to live the experience of self-giving and of the formation of an authentic human community oriented toward his final destiny, which is God."[82] God made us to be *servants first* to his creation and to one another, so a father should be a *servant first* with regard to the life of his child. Craving to be or being a *servant first* is very profound, virtuous, and spiritual because what drives it is that true human feeling of empathy.

Although the act of being a *servant first* takes place in this temporal world, its effect endures beyond this world because it involves embracing those universal human values that corre-spond to divine values as revealed in the Holy Scripture. Hence each of us experiences that internal satisfaction and justifica-tion as well as true feelings of joy and love when we reach out to others in true service for good causes; by contrast, when we desire to be *leaders first*, we are being driven by a thirst or lust for power and dominance, and we overtly create situations in which those universal human and moral values could be compromised. Therefore, only in our true servant-hood as true fathers (or mothers) here on earth can we lead our children, others, and ourselves to the discovery of the divine goodness and happiness in God.

CHAPTER SEVEN

My father gave me the greatest gift anyone
could give another person: he believed in me.
—*Jim Valvano.*

If there is anything that we wish to change in the child, we should
first examine it and see whether it is not something
that could better be changed in ourselves.
—*C. G. Jung*

The Father's Tender Human Hand in a Truth-Glove

On one graceful day, a parishioner and I had a conversation about how best to deal with children when they misbehave. He shared with me a resolution he had made: *never in his life as a father would he spank his child, no matter what the circumstances.*

Some parents might disagree with him to some degree because, for them, mild spanking is a way of disciplining a child and making the child aware that he or she did something wrong. However, I am very much inclined to agree with the parishioner. Spanking a child with the aim of discouraging bad behavior and encouraging good behavior is the equivalent of taking an instant energy drink or loads of caffeine to (stimulate the central nervous system) boost one's energy level. The effect is short-lived, and after it wears off, we are back to square one. On the other hand, when one develops the combined habits of eating the right food, exercising properly, sleeping well, and maintaining a balanced work ethic, these work together to produce sustainable energy around the clock (except in cases of ill health and disease, of course).

Therefore, from my own perceptive (and the perspectives of many child psychologists), the only sustainable way to inspire good behavior and raise a healthy, well-adjusted child is through the use of appropriate reprimands along with constant and positive life education—spiritual, human, and moral guidance as well as healthy parental examples and experiences are necessary. A combination of all these elements will begin to develop the child from within and create a sense of courage and responsibility in the child (unlike spanking and hurling harsh words, which can unfortunately spiral out of control and turn into physical abuse, creating avoidance, fear, and anger in a child). There are so many positive and effective ways to help children understand or change their behavior for the better without hitting them.

Curiously, I asked this parishioner how he had come to this resolution.

"When I was a teenager," he said, "I did something that deserved a severe punishment—the greatest mistake in my life. When my father heard about it, I thought my relationship with him was over. I thought whatever punishment he dished out to me, even if it was a very hard spanking, I would take it without question because I deserved every bit of it." As it turned out, his father called him into the room and sat him down to have a conversation. This parishioner told me he immediately fell to his knees and tearfully said to his father, "I deserve any punishment, and I am ready to embrace it with no complaint."

His father looked at him for a while and said to him (much to his disbelief), "I will not punish you, I will not condemn you, and neither will I judge you." As the parishioner, overcome with emotions, started crying, his father continued, "Just work with me. I want to help you. You are not a bad kid; you just showed terrible judgment. We can resolve all this if you just work with me."

To this day, this parishioner remains in disbelief of the love, honesty, compassion, and forgiveness his father showed him.

He came out on the other end a better person, however—without his father putting his hands on him or hurling harsh words at him that expressed abandonment, hopelessness, or rejection. That was an experience this parishioner would pass on to his own children. "When my own children make mistakes," he told me, "I might reprimand them appropriately, but I will be honest with them. But most importantly, I will let them know that there is room to grow or make changes for the better by educating and forming them with love and through my own example."

When one flees from one's humanity—which includes one's human flaws, weaknesses, and mistakes—it becomes difficult or even impossible for one to truly find inner peace or live under the internal fulfillment that proceeds from divine grace. Our Lord Jesus Christ revealed this very truth to us when he told the parable of the Pharisee and the tax collector (Luke 18:9–14). The Pharisee was in a state of denial regarding his human fallibility, weaknesses, sins, and utter dependency on the infinite grace of God. By contrast, the tax collector not only acknowledged his broken humanity, fallibility, and sins but also affirmed his total dependency on the infinite grace of God. The tax collector's humility and honesty gained him justification before God, so much so that he went home living and rejoicing in the presence of his divine mercy. Being true to our humanity means not only refusing to intentionally and continually live a debased or depraved lifestyle but also acknowledging our utter reliance on divine grace. However, embracing our broken nature is not an end in itself; rather, it is the only means by which we can come to what Christians believe is the end of our human destiny, which is living in the love and divinity of God for eternity.

After the fall of humanity from original grace to original sin, as the Holy Scripture reveals, God the Father, in his infinite love for us, sent his only son to recover and restore what had been lost, and God paid the price of his son's life and suffering for our redemption. The fundamental question is why Christ had to take on every aspect of our wounded, broken, and weak human nature except for sin. As the writer of the letter to the Hebrews explains, "He had to become like his brothers in every way, that He might be a merciful and faithful high priest before God to expiate the sins of the people. Because he himself was tested through what he suffered, he is able to help those who are being tested" (2:16–18). What this should express to us is that we should not shy away from embracing our own wounded and broken humanity. Christ's mission became one of restoration and healing of lost spiritual sight so that we could once more rediscover the goodness of God within our being, which was infused in every human from the moment of creation.

A human father has to remember that when Christ intervened in human history, he never condemned, judged, challenged, or scorned our humanity or human weaknesses. He was not ashamed of our human frailties, and he did not demand of us that we abandon our shattered and wounded natures and attempt to achieve instant perfection. Rather, out of pity, he led us through a journey of configuration and restoration and continues to lead us with that soft fatherly touch while saying, "I am aware of your brokenness; do not be afraid to pick it up and follow me, and I will make you whole again. It is only through your humanity that I can lead you to my divinity again so that you can rediscover my goodness in yourselves and others and be transformed, remade, and reconfigured into the same divine goodness, which is my image."

Human reality has proven consistently that not a single human being is perfect; rather, our wounded human nature is open to the reception of the divine grace of God, which spurs us to healing and perfection. This grace spurs us to walk the path to perfection, which comes to consummation only through Christ and in Christ when we become one with him (John 17:22–23). This road to perfection is revealed in Christ's journey with the cross to Calvary, where his love for the Father was consummated. Due to his frail humanity, he fell three times, but his divinity lifted him up again three times until his love for the Father was brought to completion.

In a human father-child relationship, the father should see his relationship with his child as a journey toward consummation in God (who is perfect), and during this journey, there are bound to be many *human-falls*. When a father in his authority witnesses these *human-falls* in his child, it is not the time for rejection and disownment, abandonment and condemnation, or judgment and preferment, and it is not the time to drive the child to despair, for "any authority, which in its exercise, drives a wrongdoer either to despair or to resentment is a failure."[83] Rather, it is the most important time for the father to extend his tender human hand with a spirit of benignity, lead his child to the truth, and help his child discover humanity's inevitable and utter dependence on the divine grace of God, through whom the child will be lifted up again and again when he or she falls. "The greatest kindness one can render to any man consists in leading him from error to truth."[84] For a father to lead his child to an understanding of this divine truth, the virtue of patience, borne out by love and wisdom, should reign.

When a father extends his tender, fatherly hand in order to lead his child on a life's journey of formation and nurturing, he should always remember the words of Robert

Greenleaf: "Acceptance of the person, though, requires a tolerance of imperfection...And the parents who try to raise perfect children are certain to raise neurotics. It is part of the enigma of human nature that the 'typical person'—immature, stumbling, inept, lazy—is capable of great dedication and heroism *if* wisely led."[85] In other words, a father who embarks on raising a perfect child is actually raising a child who will grow up incapable of embracing his or her own wounded nature and unable to sympathize or empathize with the wounded humanity of any other, breeding impatience, intolerance, and rejection.

When a child has been denied both the possibility of accepting his or her humanity in its imperfection and the "poverty of spirit," that child has also been denied the possibility of standing before God unfinished and in total emptiness so that God's perfect grace can fill the cracks in the child's wounded nature with his divine strength. This child will grow up unable to relate to others and the world around him and will sometimes even be antisocial, because here is a child who was raised to be perfect only to find himself in an imperfect world and surrounded by imperfect humans with wounded natures—how frustrating that can be!

That is why when he came to us, Christ, the Perfect One, took on our imperfect humanity and our weaknesses; instead of being frustrated with our fallen and broken nature, he was able to sympathize with us, his brothers and sisters, because he himself was like us (Hebrews 5:15). "If there is such a thing as human perfection, it seems to emerge precisely from how we handle the imperfection that is everywhere, especially our own. What a clever place for God to hide holiness, so that only the humble and the earnest will find it! A 'perfect' person ends up being one who can consciously forgive and include imperfection rather than one who thinks he or she is totally above and beyond imperfection."[86] It is the duty of a father to teach his child to understand that our human imperfection is not an end in itself but a means to perfection in God; it expresses our absolute need for the divine. So every time a child makes a mistake, it should be viewed as an opportunity for the father to step in with tender sympathy and empathy and lead the child from where he or she is to where he or she ought to be.

When a father's single goal is to form a perfect child, he will gradually start suffering from *imperfection-elimination syndrome.* This occurs when the father's entire focus is on scouting and identifying the faults in his child to the extent that the best qualities of the child, which are still in a state of potentiality, are totally ignored and, as a consequence, may never develop to fruition. By contrast, by accepting the imperfect nature of his child as a first step, a father is able to look for the smallest elements of goodness in his child and focus on them like a laser beam; thus targeting and isolating what is best in his child, he can help the child develop these great qualities. "We should see the goodness in someone, that we should communicate that to the person, who thereby is changed. The person is re-created. 'The lover creates love,' that is, sees the beauty there, and by seeing it, draws it out."[87] The father's positive attitude and belief in his child despite the son or daughter's imperfect nature helps to unleash those hidden treasures and talents that God has endowed in his child; in essence, the father then perfects creation (his child, himself, and the world) by way of the true image of God's goodness that we hold in our being.

As the father continues to give his child a chance to stand in total emptiness and imperfection before God, who is perfect, he should also give God, the divine Father, a chance to fill this emptiness with his grace and love. This would allow God to manifest his divinity and reveal his goodness as he leads this child, through the child's father, on a journey to perfection in his divine presence. However, for God to be able to fill the emptiness in a child with his divine grace and goodness, the child's human father has to first refrain from filling that emptiness himself.

CHAPTER EIGHT

Are children not already too heavily penalized by the scourge of divorce? How sad it is for a child to have to divide his love between parents in conflict! So many children will always bear the psychological scar of the suffering that their parents' separation caused them...
—*Pope John Paul II*

Fatherhood Shrouded Under the Mist of a Separation or a Divorce

One of the most distressful experiences—one that causes tremendous pain for families—is when parents walk away from marriages that were contracted in good faith and then consummated. In some cases, parents walk away not only from their marital covenant but also from each other's love and from their children, who are the visible signs and incarnations of the covenant. "The child has the right to be conceived, carried in the womb, brought into the world, and brought up within marriage: it is through the secure and recognized relationship to his [or her] own parents that the child can discover his [or her] own identity and achieve his [or her] own proper human development."[88] This inalienable right of a child to be nurtured within marriage hardly comes to some parents' minds as they face the possibility of a separation or a divorce.

Parents divorce or separate due to "irreconcilable differences" (which are, in some cases, indeed reconcilable, but one or both parties may lack the will, patience, or true forgiveness to resolve them) or because one or both parties are not truly willing to work hard and sacrifice to bring that reconciliation to fulfillment and continue living as a family; one parent might already be entangled in another relationship that is sapping the energy that should be used to heal the existing marriage. Sadly, in other cases, there might be abuse and neglect that are simply beyond human tolerance and resolve so that the only option is to encourage separation. Separation can be justifiably encouraged, when it is the only possible way of remedying the damage done to someone's human dignity and rights.

In those moments of marital crises, some couples may be so consumed by stresses that they rarely perceive the family as "a necessary good for...a great and lifelong treasure for couples, a unique good for children, who are meant to be the fruit of the love, of the total and generous self-giving of their parents."[89] Hence, for some of us in stressful and frustrating situations, the tendency to make quick decisions, be less considerate of others, and use less judgment increases; this is especially the case when we cannot wait to take flight from something we consider painful to our well-being. However, it is important and fair to note that some parents don't consider a separation or a divorce as the first option or even as an easy option, especially when they have children; for this reason they seek good pastoral and psychological care to help them when their marriages are difficult and painful.

As expressed in the Catholic Pastoral Constitution on the Church in the Modern World, "The intimate partnership of life and the love which constitutes the married state has been established by the creator and endowed by Him with its own proper laws; it is rooted in the contract of its partners, that is, in their irrevocable personal consent...For God himself is the author of marriage."[90] This understanding is undermined by what in 2002 the Pontifical Council for the Family called a *divorce mentality* — that is, the fast-growing perception by some that divorce is the only way to resolve marital difficulties despite the emotional and psychological consequences it has on children and even the couples who go through it.

The experience of a separation or a divorce is very painful and difficult and can sometimes take a very ugly turn: the divorced parents now live in disunity; instead of living in complementarity and unity, where love abounds, they now live in disunity, where sometimes competition abounds. Some divorced couples compete for everything, including acceptance, acknowledgment, and love from their children as well as physical custody of them; sadly, some of these couples now live in win-or-lose worlds. Instead of watching their marital love continue to grow and expand, as God intended, it stagnates and shrinks. "Divorce is a grave offense against the natural law. It claims to break the contract, to which the spouses freely consented, to live with each other till death. Divorce does injury to the covenant of salvation, of which sacramental marriage is the sign."[91] Even in cases of abuse, which are also offenses to divine and natural law but may justify a separation as stated, "The separation of spouses while maintaining the marriage bond can be legitimate in certain cases provided by canon law."[92] However, either a separation or a divorce still leaves us with wounded hearts and broken spirits. Our Lord Jesus Christ abrogated the *divorce law* written by Moses to emphasize to the Pharisees that the divine creator does not intend for husbands and wives to be divorced from one another. Rather, such an act was invented and is carried out because of the hardness of our hearts (Mark 10:1–12).

When a spouse, ordained to live in complementarity with his or her husband or wife, instead lives in competition and pits his or her children against the other parent while engaging in direct or indirect character assassination and castigation, he or she forces his or her children to survive by splitting their love and affection. The children are forced to apportion and ration their respect and obedience. In some cases, if the children adhere to one parent's instruction over the other's, they will incur the wrath of the other and risk falling out of their favor. According to Catholic teaching, "Divorce is immoral also because it introduces disorder into the family and into the society. This disorder brings grave harm to the deserted spouses, to children traumatized by the separation of their parents and often torn between them, and because of its contagious effect which makes it truly a plague on society."[93] In most cases, when the gravity of the effect of divorce is neglected, one of two things is bound to happen: either the father will lose the integrity of his fatherhood or the mother will lose the integrity of her motherhood. Alternatively, both parents may lose the integrity of their vocations.

This reality is self-evident in that some children in divorced families have to suffer in silence because "the very hearts of that mutual giving,"[94] which should exist between parents has been altered.

Indisputably, the *mutual giving of self* that exists between married spouses are lifelines for children—sources of strength, well-being, motivation, internal happiness, and joy. When the *mutual giving of self,* from which children spring forth, are suddenly broken and taken away due to a separation or a divorce, something essential to the harmonious well-being of the children has been infringed upon.

More significant suffering for children, surfaces in certain cases when divorced parents enter into unions with different partners. In such a case, the children are then subjected to having to accept someone new in their lives as a replacement for one of their biological parents. It is often extremely hard for the children to accept the fact that their mother is sharing her life with someone other than their father or that their father is sharing his life with someone other than their mother. The fear of the unknown and the uncertainty of being accepted by a new partner create another source of agony and suffering for the children; sometimes they vocalize it, but most times they live with it in silence. Sometimes it is also very hard for the new partner to accept children to whom he or she has no biological connection, which may lead to utter rejection, conflict, abuse, isolation, and other traumatic experiences for the children.

For this and other reasons, the children bear the greatest wounds from a divorce. "It is in fact inevitable that when the conjugal covenant is broken, those who suffer most are the children who are the living signs of its indissolubility."[95] The children feel sad, helpless, and powerless to stop the divorce. At times, this helplessness can breed internal anger.

So, when a father—because of his deep unhappiness or his feeling of hopelessness about fixing what is broken in his marriage—succumbs to the temptation to divorce, he should be mindful of all these consequences and reflect profoundly on these words of Pope John Paul II: "Dear parents, how essential it is for children to be able to count on you, on both of you—fathers and mothers—in the complementarity of your gift...Are children not already too heavily penalized by the scourge of divorce? How sad it is for a child to have to divide his love between parents in conflict! So many children will always bear the psychological scar of the suffering that their parents' separation caused them."[96] How much more pain do our children deserve? Should we as parents allow our conflicts to alter the God-given destiny of our children and even rob them of it? It will always be a disservice to the well-being and welfare of our children when separated or divorced parents live in continual conflict. In fairness to spouses, when it comes to the great suffering or distress associated with a separation or a divorce, a spouse may suffer, like the children, as a victim. However, when a custody fight drags on, it could create feelings of depression and loss that will define the couple's parental stewardship to their children, which may in turn trigger their anger or feelings of isolation and defeat. As a result, they may detach and disengage from the father-child or mother-child relationships.

One early morning in 2009, after celebrating the Eucharistic sacrifice, I walked into my office to begin the day as I did any other. On this day, however, as soon as I sat at my desk, I heard a knock on the door. When I looked through the glass of my office door, I saw a teenage girl in tears. Immediately I rose from my chair, walked to the door, and asked who she was and what was wrong.

She sat down and poured out her soul in tears about the dysfunction in her family and how it was affecting her life. Out of frustration over an altercation her parents were having, she had left her house after midnight and spent the night on the street corner. When morning came, she walked to the church, looking to talk to a priest, and found me walking to my office after Holy Mass.

Before I responded to her frustration, I said, "I understand you are very sad and hurt, but staying out at night alone by yourself on the street corner put you in a very dangerous situation. Please promise me you won't do such a thing again, no matter what the situation is."

"I promise, Father. I won't do it again," she said.

Then I began to address her frustration and pain. Her parents had been divorced, and as the only child, she had decided to stay behind with her mother since she did not have any relationship with her father (due to the way he had treated her and her mother). When her father came to visit, it usually ended in an argument. Then, while this girl was still trying to deal with the pain and sadness of her parents' divorce, her mother's new boyfriend had moved in with them. Neither the new boyfriend nor the young teenager was ready to accept the other, so they locked horns. Moreover, the girl's biological father was not happy about this new arrangement, and that created a new, triangular, conflict in which the biological father constantly got into altercations with both his ex-wife and her boyfriend; the teenager was in the middle of it all. Had there been a healthy relationship between the teenager and her biological father, she could have moved in with him; unfortunately, that was not the case.

The night the young teenager ran away from her home, she had a bitter argument with her mother's boyfriend in which her mother partially sided with her boyfriend. This infuriated the daughter, who thought the best solution was to run away from this dysfunctional situation, and she had stayed out on the street corner by herself. Imagine what could have happened to this girl. Imagine the stress and anxiety that was secretly sapping the human vigor from her life. No child wants to grow up this way.

After hearing the girl's story and comforting her, I invited her biological parents to my office for an urgent meeting, and we had a very serious conversation in which I shared with them my thoughts about what they were putting their young child through. They were very remorseful, especially the father, who started trembling and tearing up when he imagined the danger his daughter had been in by spending the night in the street by herself. He pledged before me that henceforth that he would work hard with his ex-wife to ensure their daughter's well-being, and he apologized to his daughter right at that moment. I believed his contrition was sincere but had some reservations regarding how they intended to move forward to a solution.

Divorce or separation contradicts the divine intention of God from the foundation of humanity. (According to the Catholic *Code of Canon Law,* "Marriage that is *ratum et consummatum* [ratified and consummated] can be dissolved by no human power and by no cause, except death."[97]) No child would ever wish to see his or her parents separating from or divorcing each other. However, there are certain circumstances in which separation is advised in good faith: "If either of the spouses causes grave mental or physical danger to the other spouse or to the offspring or otherwise renders common life too difficult, that spouse gives the other a legitimate cause for leaving, either by decree of the local ordinary or even on his or her own authority if there is danger in delay."[98] Separation is also advised where there is abuse that endangers the human dignity, well-being, or lives of the spouses or the children. This can include physical, moral, verbal, and psychological abuse. All abuse, no matter what form it comes in, compromises human dignity and contradicts the divine intention of God that the holy covenant of marriage should be lived out with love, complementarity, and true stewardship. For this reason, it is a moral imperative for the Christian community or society to use every tool and law (divine and human) at their disposal to put a stop to any kind of abuse (domestic, mental, marital, etc.), provided that, in using those tools or laws, honest and true moral judgments are being made.

In the midst of great suffering and anger caused by a separation or a divorce, is true human fatherhood possible? Can the human father remain entirely faithful to his fatherhood (as a steward of new life) under the cloud of misery, frustration, and loss caused by a separation or a divorce? Can the father avoid dragging the children into this conflict, or are all hopes of a true human fatherhood rendered obsolete by a broken marriage?

I would say that true human fatherhood is still possible and a father could still remain true to his fatherhood even under the shrouded mist of a separation and a divorce. Although the core element of the union is severely wounded by a separation or a divorce, it is not totally destroyed. Therefore, true human fatherhood is somewhat attainable in time of a separation or a divorce, insofar as a father is willing to claim ownership of his stewardship and is ready to humbly sacrifice and respect-fully (and consistently) work with the mother of his children out of *Christian charity*. It is morally imperative for a father to do everything in his human capacity to avoid increasing the intensity of the suffering that his children have already incurred from a separation or a divorce. In essence, causing no additional pain or suffering to the already bleeding hearts of the children is the first step in their long journey toward healing.

"Unfortunately, compared to young people from intact families, those from divorced families are more likely to lack the complex network of family and community relationships that help to propel young people into secure futures. As a con-sequence, these young people can feel isolated."[99] A father who is completely aware of this and sees his fatherhood as a divine vocation and as emanating from God should put forth a great and sincere effort to minimize or avoid complete family disintegration; such an effort would be essential for the well-being of his children. In order to achieve the goal of maintaining a family (essential to children's well-being) even in the midst of a separation or a divorce, a father should be mindful of the following elements, which I refer to as (in the words of Pope Benedict XVI) *oil on the wounds.*

WORDS AND ACTIONS THAT PROCEED FROM THE FATHER SHOULD FOSTER TRUST AND HEALING

In a post-divorce situation involving or affecting children, the father has to understand that he is now dealing with children who are internally wounded, hurting, and feeling betrayed by their own parents. He is now dealing with children who are confused about their present situation and uncertain about their futures because the most essential element in the divinely instituted human family (which generates stability, motivation, confidence, acceptance, communion, and love) has been snatched away due to their parents' decision to succumb to divorce. This essential element is *the mutual self-giving* that should exist between a father and a mother, which is intended to become a guide that introduces the children first to the true concepts of love and communion that underscore the meaning of their human nature. This is a core element ordained by God since the foundation of the world.

At the same time, as the parents allow their mutual self-giving to become a guide to love to their own children, they will successively begin to realize the final goal of the gift of themselves to each other. "In children [parents] see the crowning of their own love for each other."[100] This crowning of love is what the Second Vatican Council referred to as "the supreme gift of marriage"[101] Therefore, a child can be defined as the incarnation of the mutual giving of self between a man and a woman ordained and blessed by God. Invariably, the *mutual giving of self* between a father and a mother is an absolute necessity in the upbringing of their children, "for [it] is the right of children to be conceived within the context of total '*human self-giving*,' which is an indispensable prerequisite for their peaceful and harmonious growth."[102] This gift of self-giving between persons is divinely shared by a husband and his wife for the sole purpose of bringing to reality (through their union) the meaning of their own existence.

When this divine privilege of growing up in an atmosphere of *mutual self-giving* (between the father and the mother) is stolen from the children by divorce, they suffer. When they are deprived of being born or growing up in that communion of mutual self-giving (which guarantees stability, mutual love, acceptance, consistency, and caregiving), their natural world has undeniably been altered. Confronting his relationship with his child in this new and unnatural post-divorce world, a father must have one goal in mind: to let every word he utters and every action he displays rebuild and foster trust and heal the hurting heart of his child. This cannot replace what has been taken away, but it can mend what has been broken.

To achieve this goal, the first thing needed is *honesty*. When a father tells his child that nothing will change after a divorce except that the child will not be living with both of his or her parents in the home, he is toying with the child's emotions. The truth is that many things, if not everything, will change. "Life in a post-divorce family is very different from life in an intact family. Children who stay in contact with both parents travel back and forth between two homes, with varying sets of rules, expectations, and traditions at each place. In each place they are insiders, sharing traits and experiences with others in the household, but they are outsiders as well, because at times they look like, act like, or share experiences with the parent in the other household."[103] Imagine a child forced to live in two different homes with two different codes of conduct, while packing and unpacking backpacks most of the time. Imagine a child who will, in some cases, experience the parents fighting over who will have control over his or her well-being. Imagine, worst of all, a child being fed with deception by one parent to prevent him or her from spending more time with the other. This child has stepped into an entirely new and unnatural world, different from the one in which his or her parents were in the midst of mutual self-giving. Even when some of these cited instances of parenting dysfunction do not occur, it is still difficult for the child because he or she is not living with both parents in the home.

The more a father is able to stand by the side of his child in full presence and honestly and prudently explain (in a way that is comprehensible to his child, with consideration for his or her level of understanding and emotional maturity) the sad but true reality that may surface as an aftereffect of divorce without scaring or frightening the child, the more helpful he will be to his child. By being truthful in this manner, the father helps the child prepare emotionally, mentally, psychologically, and socially as he or she confronts a new *unnatural world invented by the parents* that is devoid of *mutual self-giving*. Despite their emotional and psychological fragility, children can be very resilient in dealing with difficult situations when they receive positive support and witness their parents behaving positively.

A father should avoid keeping his child in suspense or surprising his child with regard to his own post-divorce life, for children are apt to feel betrayed in an environment where surprises become routine. Surprises do not help to foster trust and healing. A father has to be proactive in communicating and listening in the true spirit of dialogue; truly listening provides evidence of the father's ability to *fully identify himself* with spoken words and the bearers of those words. In this fashion, the father should allow his child to participate fully in his life just as he should participate fully in the life of his child. Depending on the psychological and emotional maturity of the child, the extent of participation may vary; when a father makes certain decisions that are necessary for himself but that will directly affect the well-being of his child, however, the child has the right to be aware of them and to have relevant and well-considered input according to his or her level of maturity.

I am not suggesting that the father should tell the child everything about his private life or about every decision he makes with regard to the well-being of the child (which may create too much of an emotional burden or too much anxiety). Rather, I am advocating for the father to give the child a sense of participation in his or her own life destiny — a great recipe for healthy emotional and psychological growth and strong self-esteem. In other words, I believe that there are certain things the father should proactively communicate to his child while still maintaining a healthy boundary between himself and his child. The father has to prudently convey the necessary issues at the level of maturity and understanding of his child.

A child needs to know the truth about certain necessary changes that will come after a separation or a divorce and the sacrifices that both his or her father and the child will have to make; dialogue should become the password into the child's heart. By creating open avenues of dialogue, a father will foster a less intense environment where both he and his child are able to grow in their trust for each other so that the child will be able to express pains and joys as well as worries and concerns with the expectation that he or she will be listened to; also, a father also has to understand that his child is affected by divorce. Even when a child does not verbally express it, he or she is internally hurting, feeling a sense of loss and betrayal in the knowledge that something has been taken away. The child has lost that *divinely ordained complementarity that is meant to exist between a father and a mother and that fosters their child's harmonious well-being.* Therefore, the father has to be cautious and act with a great deal of prudence and patience in relation to his children to avoid escalating the pain and agony that has been inflicted by the parents who have divorced.

PARENTING SHOULD REMAIN A MATTER OF SHARED, EQUAL, AND JOINT CUSTODY AND RESPONSIBILITY

When a father goes to the extreme of voluntarily relinquishing the shared equal custody of his child solely to the mother and takes on the status of a noncustodial father for convenient or avoidable reasons, he has given himself *the* status of a *visiting father*; that is, instead of being truly present and remaining a vital and indispensable part of the life of his child, as intended by God from the foundation of creation, he has freely placed himself in a situation in which he gradually becomes a *dispensable commodity*. When a father freely gives up his stewardship and deserts his vocation only to become a *visiting father*, he invariably gives up his fatherhood. As it is said in the Acts of the Apostles, "Let his encampment become desolate...and may another take his office."[104] Within a short period of time, he will start to become less relevant to his child so that even his occasional physical presence will not make much difference—the child has been formed by his consistent absence.

This opens the door for someone other than the father to step in and take his place. A child who comes to the realization that his or her life is indeed going to be devoid of a father presence and at the same time sees his or her peers enjoying the presence, confidence, and support that a father gives would likely have no other option but to search (either consciously or unconsciously) for a father figure to fill the void. This is simple human dynamics: vacuums must be filled one way or another, whether positively or negatively. Even when the opportunity to fill a vacuum has not presented itself, the search continues, intentionally or unintentionally.

Similarly, when a father has been denied equal custody (which entails responsibility) of his children, either by state law or because the child demands that the mother be his or her custodial parent, there is a substantial implication that prior to the separation or the divorce and custody court hearing there had been a *defect in his fatherhood*. His fatherhood was likely missing many of the essential elements of true stewardship when it came to its correspondence with the divine Fatherhood of God. This is the kind of fatherhood that a child probably does not wish to continue to experience, so a divorce or a separation may become for a child, what Elizabeth Marquardt calls a "necessary remedy."[105]

Despite the fact that the Church states in the Catechism of the Catholic Church that *divorce is immoral*, the Church, also (with great sadness and pain) states, "If civil divorce remains the only possible way of ensuring certain legal rights, the care of the children, or the protection of inheritance, it can be tolerated and does not constitute a moral offense."[106] For that reason, a divorce or a separation can become a *necessary imperfection* to get out of an *unnecessary nightmare*—the father's unhealthy presence (according to the Catholic teachings, despite the fact that a divorce has a standing before the state, for a validly married couple it does nothing to nullify the bond of their sacramental marriage).

When a father's absence becomes a *necessary remedy* for the well-being of his child, a profound and honest reflection and evaluation on the part of the father regarding his ability to truthfully live out his divine vocation and fulfill his stewardship of the divine gift of his child is called for.

By contrast, when a father remains faithful to his fatherhood from the onset and allows his fatherhood to become a true reflection of the divine Fatherhood of God even when the sad tragedy of divorce breaks the bond of mutual self-giving in love, the child will still accept him and want his presence to continue to reign in his or her life. In these cases, the father's presence becomes as vitally important as the mother's. It would therefore be uncharitable for a father to assume that a divorce between the spouses always results in an indirect divorce between him and his child as well and makes it necessary for him to take on the status of a *visiting father*. He has to understand that it is both a natural and inalienable human right for every child to have a father who is ceaselessly and fully present in his or her life.

A father who remains cognizant of this truth and lives by it opens the door for his child to holistically participate in the father's life, no matter what the circumstances may be. "The man and the woman must assume together, before themselves and before others, the responsibility for the new life which they have brought into existence."[107] It takes two to generate a new life, and it will take two to intently watch this new life grow. Even if they are divorced, both father and mother have the shared responsibility of raising their child, and the child has the inalienable right to have a healthy relationship with both parents. At the same time, each of the parents should allow the child to have a healthy relationship with the other parent, insofar as there is no abuse. However, when one party, for no grave reason but just for convenience (or for material or financial reasons), demands full custody of a child, with only visitation rights granted to the other party, this is a recipe for disconnection and deprivation. It leads to the same sad human phenomenon of a father's absence from his child's life.

Unless there is a grave reason or a danger to the well-being of their child, both the father and the mother should have equal custody and responsibility for the sacred life they jointly brought into this world. A father leaving behind his child to the sole care and responsibility of the mother (although it is true that many mothers are fully capable of nurturing their children in the absence of a father) contradicts the divine intention of God as it pertains to his gift of new life. This is the divine intention of God: "The newborn child gives itself to its parents by the very fact of its coming into existence. Its existence is already a gift, the first gift of the Creator to the creature."[108] Fundamentally, the father has to remember that his child is not a *dispensable property* but a sacred gift given to him by God in complementarity with the mother. This gift of life was ordained to be nurtured, loved, protected, and cared for, not only by one of the spouses but by *both* spouses, who are the recipients of this divine gift of life by virtue of their mutual self-giving in sexual complementarity.

THERE SHOULD BE MUTUAL SELF-RESPECT BETWEEN SEPARATED OR DIVORCED SPOUSES

There is an unresolved mystery in my own family about which, even to this day, my mother refuses to comment. From the moment, I became aware of my own existence and until my father died, I never witnessed (or at least I cannot remember witnessing) my parents arguing, quarrelling, or even making negative comments about each other. This always baffled me, as they are both humans with flaws, weaknesses, and limitations, and they were certainly upset with each other at various points in their lives.

One day, dissatisfied with my unreliable memory on this issue, I called together my siblings and asked them if they could help me to remember any time that our parents argued or quarreled. After all of us recollected the past, we came back to the present with empty hands and minds. Many years after my father died, I asked my mother in the presence of my siblings, "Did you and Dad ever in your married life have any misunderstandings or quarrels?" To my greatest disappointment, however, she grinned (so cheerfully that I knew something was amiss) and said to me, "Son, my relationship with my husband is none of your business" — which drew huge laughter from my siblings.

I know without any doubt that, by virtue of my parents' humanity, they must have had misunderstandings and conflicts. However, they must have made a pact lasting their lifetimes not to speak ill of each other in our presence and to keep their misunderstandings and arguments far away from us. So they must have argued only when my siblings and I were out or asleep or in situations when both of them were alone. Another pact they must have made was to work together at all times on our upbringing. When any of my siblings or I misbehaved as children, we would receive appropriate reprimands from both my father and my mother at the same time. For instance, if my father was the one reprimanding us for bad behavior, my mother would support him, and vice versa, therefore leaving no division between them for us to exploit. So they succeeded in presenting and leaving to our memory only their unabridged unity, complementarity, and consistent mutual respect when it came to their relationship with us.

The effect of these experiences was that my siblings and I grew up unable to say that we loved either parent more than the other. Our love for them is equally shared and proportioned. There is no greater feeling of inner peace, joy, and empowerment for a child than to live in the midst of parents who relate as a person and work in a spirit of Christian charity with the goal of letting love reign, even in the most difficult moments or during disagreements. By virtue of our humanity, we are bound to make mistakes; when we acknowledge them, we usher in the virtue of humility, which is essential to our betterment.

Hence, when parents mistakenly voice their utter frustration or anger toward each other in the presence of their children, it is very important for the children's well-being (since they witnessed the conflict) to also witness their parents' journey to reconciliation through healthy dialogue. In this manner, the children learn conflict management from their parents and begin to see conflict and discord not as the norm but as loosed threads in the woven fabric of a healthy relationship that needs to be rewoven again and again. Parents can only take their children through their journey from conflict to reconciliation and understanding with mutual self-respect, which is absolutely necessary in every good act of conflict management and, furthermore, fundamental to raising psychologically healthy children.

A father once told me in a marriage-counseling session that he never realized how much he was hurting his young daughter when he engaged in argument or disagreement with his wife. One evening after his relationship with his wife had greatly improved, he was taking a walk with his daughter, who at one point held his hand and said, "Daddy, when you and Mom get along, that makes me happy."

The father was at a loss for words. He had been totally unaware of the effect his contentious relationship with his wife was having on his daughter. Ashamed of his lack of awareness, the only words the father could utter were apologies to the daughter with the promise that he would never again hurt her through his unhealthy interactions with his wife. He made a decision to always reconcile and forgive in moments of misunderstanding; henceforth he would do his utmost to get along with his wife. Blessed is this child, for she was able to experience her parents getting along as well as not and then voice her preference. Think about all the other children who do not have the same courage to speak out but instead just suffer in silence.

When a husband and wife (or even divorced spouses) make an honest and sincere decision to relate to each other as persons and refrain from speaking ill of each other or arguing before their children, especially in difficult times of misunderstanding, what ensues is *mutual self-respect*, which is something that every child has a right to. The mutual self-respect that should exist between a husband and wife (and even divorced spouses) eventually becomes vital to the well-being of a child. "If hostility is frequent and/or severe... the result can be traumatizing to the children...As a result, when they become aware of the feeling of hostility between parents, it creates internal dissonance for the children. That is, they feel stressed when either parent is under attack for whatever reason...When children repeatedly witness hostility between their parents, they often feel impotent...From impotent, is not too far to rage...It interrupts important child development tasks."[109] For these reasons, what children want most from their parents besides love is for them to mutually respect each other, even if they are divorced. Obviously, children do not wish to see their parents fighting, arguing, or undermining each other's credibility or character by talking negatively about each other. It is important to note that having mutual self-respect does not mean that disagreements or differences in opinion should be absent but rather that, in the event of disagreements, parents should come to compromises that are reasonable, workable, and human. It is also very important to note that compromise, in the context of *mutual self-respect*, entails being open to the other's point of view and possibly accepting what the other suggests as a better option or solution.

Mutual self-respect between divorced or separated spouses is not a substitute for the *mutual giving of self in love*, because it is only a part of a whole; it is just a single branch on a whole tree. In the midst of divorce, the *mutual giving of self*, which is a whole, is wounded and broken, and one of the elements that constitute this union is *mutual self-respect*. As the father stands before this wounded state, one thing he should try to retrieve as quickly as possible from the rubble of a broken marriage is the *respect for the mother of his child as a person with human dignity in its purity and as an image of God.*

BOTH PARTIES SHOULD FOSTER AN UNBROKEN AND UNABRIDGED CONTINUITY OF TRUE FATHERHOOD

Commenting on the *necessity of the incarnation* (Christ taking human flesh) in his Sermon on the Nativity of Christ, Pope Leo the Great stated, "Unless he was God, He would not have brought a remedy, and unless He was human, He would not have set an example."[110] In his human exemplification, Christ revealed a character of constancy and unabridged continuity in the divine Fatherhood of God, which flows from within his being, is unconditioned by anything outside of himself, endures human weaknesses and faults, and is not deterred by misfortune and tragedy. He becomes more present even when humanity ignores him, for his divine Fatherhood is persistent, and it is the same Fatherhood from which all human fatherhood emanates. This constancy in the divine Fatherhood of God is evident from these words of the psalmist in Holy Scripture: "[God] remembers forever his covenant, the pact imposed for a thousand generations, which was made with Abraham, confirmed by oath to Isaac, and ratified as binding for Jacob, an everlasting covenant for Israel."[111] This reinforces the central message of the parable of the prodigal son, in which the father of the prodigal son remained faithful to his fatherhood and fatherly love even when his son willingly strayed from that love.

Every divine vocation or call to stewardship is simply the grace of God building on human nature. Therefore, at the foundation of humanity, God ordained every divine vocation to be a *covenant* between God and humanity; the agreement was that *the perfection of our humanity could be found through a revelation of his divinity*. This covenant remains in place until both parties have fulfilled their sides of the pact; even when the human party breaks this covenant, the divine party remains faithful and waits for the human party to come back to it. When a man and a woman say yes to the vocation of parenthood and to the stewardship of a new gift of life by contracting marriage and consummating that marriage through sexual complementarity, they have willingly and automatically entered into a covenant with God. This is the divine part of that covenant, as God would express it: *I shall perfect your humanity as you extend my divinity through my divine gift of life in your child.*

In essence, the child becomes the visible sign of that covenant between the married couple and God. So even when a married couple decides to break their own covenant of marriage, which they freely made in good faith before God, the covenant that they automatically entered into with God when they consummated their marriage should not in any way be broken. This covenant is ordained to remain unabridged because the new life they have created is divinely and naturally ordained to utterly depend on his or her parents until maturity. This implies that every father and mother will render an account of his or her faithfulness and fulfillment of his or her pact with God.

As I stated before, procreation by itself does not result in true human fatherhood; rather, the combination of procreation and unabridged continuity in nurturing, educating, leading, and caring for that new life is what causes true human fatherhood. This unabridged continuity in a father-child relationship comes with dual rewards, as Pope Benedict XVI wrote:

For the inner relationship of the family to be complete, they [a father and a mother] also need to say a "yes" of acceptance to the children whom they have given birth to or adopted, and each of which has his or her own personality and character. In this way, children will grow up in a climate of acceptance and love, and upon reaching sufficient maturity, will then want to say "yes" in turn to those who gave them life.[112]

A true father's children will be beside him in his old age when weakness overwhelms his physical and mental existence. He will not be perturbed, because his children will surround him with pure love. When he is in need of help, he will have many loving hands reaching out to him, not out of duty but out of love.

This remains true no matter how effectively a divorced father puts all these *constituent elements that are essential* (continual nurturing, educating, leading, and caring for the new life) into use; the *core essential element — mutual giving of self in love —* which was ordained by God to fully exist between a husband and wife, would still be lacking in his journey to true human fatherhood. These *constituent and essential elements* can go a long way toward helping children of divorced parents begin to minister to the *wounds inflicted on them by their parents.* By the infinite grace of God and with the help of good friends, acquaintances, and relatives, they can begin to take their destiny and well-being into their own hands.

In some human circumstances, children are unable to reach that stage in adulthood in which they are able to give freely to another new life (which they have generated) all that was denied or taken from them by their own parents. They might be forced to turn to cynicism and adopt a negative outlook on a life of parenting or marriage. This can be a result of the severity of a divorce—and the accompanying *wounds that were inflicted by the parents*—that they experienced as children post-divorce.

Understanding this very sad reality faced by many innocent children, Pope Benedict XVI expressed the necessity of seeking a strong and durable link between the children of divorced parents and their parents. Advising the members of the mystical body of Christ—the church—and the family on matters of marriage and family, he placed before us an enormous responsibility: "Supportive pastoral attention must therefore aim to ensure that the children are not the innocent victims of conflicts between parents who divorce. It must also endeavor to ensure that the continuity of the link with their parents is guaranteed as far as possible, as well as the links with their own family and social origins, which are indispensable for a balanced psychological and human growth."[113] Therefore, when a married couple divorces, neither parent is in any way also entitled to walking away from his or her vocation as steward of the lives he or she has produced through divine creative acts. A durable, strong, and unbroken relationship with his or her children should never be compromised. We have to remember that every life given to us by God will be accounted for before him.

Watching Me Grow Up

When nature takes away the warmth of my mother's womb,
will you be there to watch me cry my first cry? Daddy!
Will you watch over me, when I take my first sleep?

I may know of you not at first, but will
I feel your hands holding mine,
as the warmth from your hands runs through my veins
and brings me comfort, as you watch me grow?
When I take my first walk on earth,
will you be there to hold me when I am about to fall?
I know you will watch me grow.

Ah! I want to see how you feel when I smile.
I want to see how you feel when I am sad.
Will I hear your voice waking me up in the morning
as it mingles with the voices of the early-morning birds
that sing and express their admiration to their maker?

Will I hear your voice gently fade into the night
with the hoots of the tawny owls
as you read to me my favorite night story?

When I grow up and begin my own voyage of life,
I shall ask one of my little Angels to watch over you until I am back,
for all the moments that you watch me grow to maturity, I
shall never forget.
Aha! I shall watch over you now, as you live life to the fullest.

—*Faustinus Uchenna Anyamele.*

CHAPTER NINE

*When I talk of forgiveness I mean the belief that you can come out
the other side a better person. A better person than the one being
consumed by anger and hatred. Remaining in that state locks you in
a state of victimhood, making you almost dependent on the perpetrator. If you can find it in yourself to forgive then you are no longer
chained to the perpetrator.*

—*Archbishop Desmond Tutu*

A Father Giving in Full Measure What he was Denied

In the early summer of 2007 in Aurora, Colorado, I met Mr.
Jay, a very intelligent man, father, and grandfather. He is also
a man of many books—reading is his passion. In the ensuing
years, we have developed a great friendship. We share ideas
and talk about many things, although most often about books.
Whenever I speak with him on the phone, the first thing he asks

me about is what new book I've been reading. To be candid, most of the time I have no answer, because I can hardly keep up with him.

Although we have been friends for the past years, I never knew that this intelligent, engaging, well-rounded father and grandfather had a childhood secret. He didn't reveal it until I sent this very manuscript to him. The next day I called him by phone to make sure he had received the document.

"Yes, I received your e-mail," he said, "but when I opened the document and saw the title, I could not believe it: *The Father They Wish to Have.* I am very curious about the contents of this book, but it may be hard for me to read through."

"Is it about the title or the whole work in general?" I asked.

"It is about me and my childhood," he said. "When I saw the title, I just had a feeling that this manuscript would stir things up in my life, things I have kept to myself and wanted to keep to myself."

"I am very sorry to hear that," I said. Out of curiosity, I asked, "Is it something you don't mind sharing with me? If you wish not to, I would definitely understand."

"Well," he said, "I know I have never said this to you before, but the truth is that, as a child, I had no father. I was born out of wedlock and grew up never knowing my father till later in life."

I paused for a moment, trying to decide if I should go ahead and ask more questions or if I should call it off to avoid bringing to the present painful memories of his childhood. "Would you like to share with me what your experiences were then and what they are now," I asked, "especially now that you are a father and a grandfather?"

"Sure, but there are not a lot of positive things I can offer you," he said.

"That's all right," I said. "If you don't mind giving me what you have, negative or positive, I think there would be something I could learn from it."

Mr. Jay and I had dinner together the following week, and he poured out to me the sad memories of his childhood and the experience of growing up as a teenager with no father figure. Despite how happy he is today as a father and grandfather, I could still hear the undertones of his frustrating childhood when he shared with me his experience of a very low self-esteem as a young boy, which was a result of not being able to talk confidently about his own father or family among his friends. Whenever they asked him, "How about your father?" all he said was, "I do not know." In addition, he was left in an emotional limbo about his own family history; you could see the sadness in his heart reflected in his facial expressions.

He told me that when he asked his mother if he had a father, she dismissively said that she and his father got an annulment, and that was all.

As a young adult, Mr. Jay revisited this issue again, pleading with his mother to tell him the truth, and that was when he found out that he was born out of wedlock and would never have a father presence in his life. That was devastating. Another astonishing revelation to him was that the person Mr. Jay had referred to, as his grandmother was not actually his biological grandmother but a woman who had compassionately taken in his mother when she was pregnant with him. Hence, throughout his childhood and the early stages of his teenage life, Mr. Jay's family history had been a puzzle to him; he was confused and left guessing when it came to his natural relationships and links with the people around him.

His mother later married a man whom Mr. Jay called his stepfather, but they had an unhealthy relationship. According to Mr. Jay, the stepfather was sometimes abusive to his mother and paid hardly any attention to him as a boy, which created a chasm between them. Mr. Jay went further to say that, as a child and teenager, there was negligible affection in his family, and the stepfather was drunk most evenings. He said he was very sad back then and had low self-esteem. "I tried to deal with this situation by staying away from home a lot," he said. "I stayed at

my friends' houses with their parents, and that was very helpful for me as a young teenager."

These childhood and teenage experiences caused great pain
and sadness for Mr. Jay, especially when he witnessed his peers
growing up in happy and loving families, in which both parents
remained present with their children at all times—this made him
feel all the more saddened for all that had been denied him. So,
to fill the vacuum of affection, love, and presence he had been left
with from the absence of a true father figure, he decided to spend
most of his time as a teenager visiting and staying at the homes
of these friends to experience what a functional family looked
and felt like. Mr. Jay went into detail about his experience, and
the more I listened to him, the more I could picture him as a boy
who refused to give up and feel sorry for himself.

When I asked if he was still angry about how his childhood
was stolen from him, he said he wasn't. "After a while," he said,
"it became clear to me that anger is not a solution. Nor would it
ever be a solution to anything, past, present or even that which
is to come."

Hence, as a way of bringing healing to his sad childhood, he
started looking at the positive side of life.

When, as an adult, he became a father himself, he made sure
to have new and healthy experiences with his own children, based

on what he had learned as a teenager while watching and spending a lot of time with families of his friends. "I believed that what I experienced with these families back then," he said, "was true and pure, because I felt better and more serene when I was welcomed and accepted into such families with great affection. I am not a perfect father, but I try to give to my children all the good and positive things that I was denied as a child and as a young boy."

As Mr. Jay began to take a new direction, he forgave and forgot his sad experiences of a father-deprivation. Forgetting in this context is what Clarissa Pinkola Estes calls "conscious forgetting", "willfully dropping the practice of obsessing, intentionally outdistancing and losing sight of it, not looking back, thereby living in a new landscape, creating new life and new experiences to think about instead of the old ones. This kind of forgetting does not erase memory, it lays the emotion surrounding the memory to rest."[114] Most of the time, it is the experience of both happy and sad moments in one's life that conditions one's present and helps fashion one's future. The positive memories in one's life are worth holding on to, even though the sad memories persist. When we try to block out the painful memories, the emotions that come with them can be tamed by the virtuous act of true forgiveness on our part, creating new memories and by tapping into a positive attitude.

At a critical moment in his life, Mr. Jay understood that he could not change his sad past. Therefore, he decided to embrace it with a determination to look forward to a better future. Taking a journey back into himself, Mr. Jay tapped into his interior attitude, and he found the will to live, to be a survivor, and to believe again. He started feeding on the positive experiences with father figures and functional families (families of his friends) he had had as a teenager. As a father, he started creating healthy and positive memories of father-child relationships by being active in his relationships with his children. After a period of time, these new positive memories of father-child relationships became dominant, causing the sad memories to recede. Sometimes, even for Mr. Jay, these older, *bitter, recessive memories* are still triggered by present events. For example, he related to me that his sad experience of his father's deprivation was once triggered by scenes from the movie *Field of Dreams.* When this occurs, Mr. Jay can put to rest the emotions surrounding his older memories by invoking the newer memories of his healthy father-child relationships.

Mr. Jay's reactions to his regrettable childhood experiences reveal contradictory ways of dealing with traumatic experiences of deprivation, denial, and abuse. One option is to continue to live with the status of *victimhood*, which means living under the shadow of one's sadness and painful experiences and allowing them to rule one's present life. This is not where God wishes us to be, because this approach to life's adversities not only empowers the perpetrator but also builds up resentment, anger, rage, depression, and frustration—a continuous bleeding within our hearts.

People who live in victimhood constantly feel that something has been taken away from them that will never be returned. They feel emptiness within themselves that anger quickly fills unless it is replaced with the grace of forgiveness and an inward resolve to reclaim the joys of life. A human father who was, as a child, robbed of the right of a father's presence and love, or who was abused by the one who was supposed to be his true father, might choose to maintain a status of victimhood, which only continues to empower the victimizer while vanquishing the victim. Archbishop Desmond Tutu, in his "Talk on Forgiveness" (which was given in relation to South African apartheid), made this matter so clear when he wrote the following:

> When I talk of forgiveness, I mean the belief that you can come out the other side a better person. A better person than the one being consumed by anger and hatred. Remaining in that state locks you in a state of victimhood, making you almost dependent on the perpetrator. If you can find it in yourself to forgive then you are no longer chained to the

perpetrator. You can move on, and you can even help the perpetrator to become a better person too.[115]

In essence, when we make the choice to remain victims, which only gives acclaim to the perpetrators, we rob from ourselves our will to journey into lives that are worth living.

The second approach, which is better, healthier, and more fruitful, is to begin to live as a *survivor*. This begins when we take a forgiving approach to the bitter experiences associated with the deprivation, absence, abuse, or neglect of our fathers. This means living above and beyond the pains of our past inhumane experiences, being in total control of our inner emotions, and tapping into our *inner attitudes* to live happily again and experience that pure inner happiness of gratitude to God for what he has given to us. This choice goes a long way toward saving us from depression, posttraumatic stress, anger, unwillingness to forgive, and, in extreme cases, revenge. Like Mr. Jay, a father who was denied the true presence of a father in his own childhood can begin to empower himself from within by actually being present in his own child's life and by giving in full measure to his child what was denied to him in the past, thereby creating new memories in a father-child relationship.

Through my own experiences, I discovered that, in our God-given lives, there is no better therapy or medicine for inner healing than the power within our souls with which God has infused us from the foundation of our humanity. Waiting for the world outside of our beings to bring us inner peace would be like waiting for a male dog to lay an egg. The world and its occupants can cause tremendous pain, leaving us hurting and broken. We could become our own enemies and cause ourselves a great deal of pain by wrongly answering to life's realities or by pursuing temporary and superficial satisfactions to fill a permanent yearning for inner happiness, healing, or reconciliation within ourselves. On such occasions, we think that the antidote to our inner pains is outside of us, not knowing that the only antidote that can bring true healing and reconciliation is deep within our being, waiting for us to activate it. All we have to do is freely and willingly (and courageously) reach inside ourselves and harness that divinely infused antidote to our past or present pain.

That is fundamentally what professional therapists help their patients do, especially those patients who are unable to reach inside themselves on their own for this true antidote to human existential pain, perhaps due to the severity of their past experiences. The professional therapist helps us reach into our inner selves and harness that power of positivity and healing (the will to live again and to better our lives) that God himself intentionally created in us.

Because God, our creator, knows that there will be hardship and pain in our lives, he placed his power and grace within us to be accessed on such occasions. So the power of our healing is within us, and all we need is the human will and divine grace to tap into it.

For example, a father who, in childhood, was denied the real presence of his own father can begin to heal by journeying back into himself. First, he can acknowledge his frustration, resentment, and pain that were the result of father-deprivation and neglect. Second, he can seek counseling, either psychological or pastoral, in a process of true forgiveness. Third, he can proceed courageously, taking himself on a spiritual journey toward a true act of forgiveness. He might begin such a journey by making a list of all that he was deprived of as a child, whether out of the culpable ignorance, chronic self-absorption, or flagrant inhumanity of his father. This is what I would refer to as the *father-deprivation list*. Here are some examples of what kinds of details might be added to the list:

- I was denied a father figure as a child, and consequently have no concept of what it means to have a father.
- I was denied a father who used his authority for good rather than to justify constant abuse and humiliation.

- I was denied the experience of having a holistic father's presence; in other words, I had a partial father's presence (he had the status of a *visiting father*) or no father presence at all.
- I was denied a father who administered true justice (a justice that was endured or absorbed in mercy).
- I was denied a father who did not ration his love by preferment.
- I was denied a father's attention and instead had a father who focused squarely on his own personal interests and pleasures.
- I was denied the kind of mutual giving of self that was divinely ordained to exist between a father and a mother (I grew up in a divorced family).
- I was denied that foundation in life to which every child has a right in order to confront this complex world and its realities.

After making such a list, the father may, of his own accord, give back to his child in full measure all that was deprived of him. When he is able to do so, he can create new memories in a father-child relationship. At the same time, he will bring healing to his own heart and joy into the life of his child. That is what it means to reach within oneself and harness that divinely infused power that will turn one from being a victim (due to past deprivation) into being a survivor and enable one to conquer adversities; this is *organic self-therapy.* This power of healing comes from within our souls and the cores of our beings.

This gradual process of internal movement from the bitter memories of the past to the creating of positive experiences in the present is what Pope John Paul II referred to as *the purification of memory.* "Purifying the memory means eliminating from personal and collective conscience all forms of resentment or violence left by the inheritance of the past... which becomes the foundation for a renewed moral way of acting."[116] In other words, purifying ones memory is not the elimination of the memory. Rather, it is the disposition to give internal healing a chance by consistently and willfully creating and feeding our consciousness with new positive experiences that will gradually begin to nullify the emotional (physical and psychological) effect of unhealthy memories. *Purifying of memory* can be applied to the hurtful memories of father-deprivation or to the pain that comes from our own denials, deprivations, and mistakes. The pain from these memories may have been inherited by us, directly inflicted on us by others; or inflicted by us through our own wrongful judgments or human errors.

When a father engages in this exercise of purifying of the memory, it is important for him to understand that is not in any way a deletion of past bitter experiences. Rather, it is the foundation for true healing and forgiveness of past wrongs committed against him. Therefore, the father's *consistent, willful, gradual, and pragmatic creation and feeding of his consciousness with new and positive experiences of a father-child relationship in the present for the future—an antidote to negative memories*—fosters the elimination of resentment (due to unhealthy memories) from his *personal* and *collective consciences*. In due time, as new and positive memories are created, the negative memories gradually recede, and even if they are triggered by events of the present or by the recounting of history, they will not be psychologically, spiritually, emotionally, or physically lethal to him—because they are no longer dominant.

Failing to take this proactive approach to creating new positive memories would leave a father with the past bitterness of father-deprivation or denial still in his heart. This would be a recipe for elongated anger and resentment, which might rob him of a healthy father-child relationship in the present and threaten the future. Altogether, it would make life unworthy of living when it comes to his own relationship with his child.

However, we have to acknowledge that not every man who has engendered a child can raise his child or be present with his child. Some men lack a fundamental understanding of themselves, their identities, and their abilities. Some men are incapable of crafting spousal relationships with their wives, with whom they bear responsibility for bringing new lives into the world and nourishing those new lives into adulthood. Such an inability always emerges as a tragedy in a family, and it may cause a father to abandon his children and wife or to intoxicate himself to cover for real or perceived personal inadequacies and dysfunctions that have plagued him from his own childhood through his adolescence and adulthood. Obviously, children suffer in the wake of such a parental tragedy.

There are no formational opportunities for would-be husbands and fathers other than personal experience followed by mature reflection and a desire to be a servant and a leader of one's own children for their benefit. Sadly, there are some men who are so chronically self-absorbed or distracted that they are unable to be sufficiently altruistic for marriage and family. Still, there are some men whose own rearing was severely damaged, to the extent that it offered no model or inspiration for their own fathering. These are the tragic realities we have to continuously grapple with when the human person willfully takes upon himself or herself the journey of life without the author of life—God and his divine grace.

CONSUMMATION

The last end is the first principle of being, in which
all perfection is preserved, and toward whose likeness all
things strive according to their perfection.
—*Saint Thomas Aquinas.*

The Consummation

Christians believe that our human journey to perfection by grace is consummated when we finally become one with God in his likeness. "Everything that strives after its own perfection tends towards likeness to God."[117] A human, therefore, can achieve perfection only when all of his or her human actions (*actus humanus*) honor the invitation to participate in the spirit of divine perfection of God through imitation of the person of Christ.

Without denigrating the positive effect of sincere human efforts, it must be said that they are inadequate in and of themselves (without divine grace) to bring us to that perfection.

"While the human being did indeed receive the dignity of God's image in the first creation, the dignity of his likeness is reserved for the consummation…For in the beginning only the possibility of perfection is given them by the dignity of the 'image,' while in the end, they are to acquire for themselves the perfect 'likeness' by the carrying out of works [through grace]."[118]

In essence, the act of true human fatherhood, which is a divine vocation and a virtuous act aimed toward perfection in the likeness of the supreme Fatherhood of God, never comes to fulfillment until we come face-to-face with God the Father, from whom all human fatherhood emanates, and render a full account of our fatherly stewardship. As Christians believe, the human being has been divinely ordained with a destiny that ends back at its source or origin: "The emanation of creatures from God would be imperfect unless they returned to Him in equal measure."[119] Hence, when God made us, he destined us to reunite with him again. Therefore, he planted in us a variety of seeds (vocations, talents, and gifts) to carry into the world and the human family, which have the potential to bear good fruits if used unselfishly. These good fruits are what God intends us to return to him.

Until that moment when our humanity comes to consummation in God through Christ, true human fatherhood will not cease, for its finality is not determined by the legal age or maturity of a child. Rather, fatherhood is a divine vocation for life, ordained to be enriched and to be fruitful in due time, until it comes to consummation in the divine Fatherhood. In this pure moment, true human fathers will hear the divine affirmation of the true stewardship of their human fatherhood—*these are my beloved sons, who lived out their human fatherhood in accordance with my divine will*—and invariably this will make them like Christ himself. Every human father should remember always the words of Meister Eckhart: "Every...man, woman and child has a soul and it is the destiny of all, to see as God sees, to know as God knows, to feel as God feels, to be as God Is."[120]

Notes

1 Psalm 127:3.

2 John Paul II, *Familiaris consortio* [Apostolic Exhortation] (November 22, 1981), 25.

3 National Fatherhood Initiative, *"The Father Factor"* http://www.fatherhood.org/media/consequences-of-father-absence-statistics (accessed January 13, 2013).

4 "Children's Living Arrangements and Characteristics," table C8 (Washington, DC: US Census Bureau, March 2011).

5 Cynthia C. Harper and Sara S. McLanahan, "Father Absence and Youth Incarceration," *Journal of Research on Adolescence* 14 (September 2004): 369–397.

6 Christine Winquist Nord and Jerry West, *Fathers' and Mothers' Involvement in Their Children's Schools by Family Type and Resident Status* (Washington, DC: US Department of Education, National Center for Education Statistics, 2001).

7 Laura L. Garcia, "Authentic Freedom and Equality in Difference," *Women, Sex, and the Church: A Case For Catholic Teaching*, ed. Erika Bachiochi (Boston: Pauline Books & Media, 2010), 17.

[8] James M Herzog, *Father Hunger: explorations with adults and children (Analytic Press, Inc.* 2001), 22.

[9] Genesis 2:8.

[10] John Paul II, *Familiaris consortio*, 14.

[11] Jeffner Allen, "Motherhood: The Annihilation of Women," in *Mothering: Essays in Feminist Theory*, ed. Joyce Trebilcot (Totowa, NJ: Rowman & Allanheld, 1983), 316.

[12] Saint Thomas Aquinas, *Summa contra gentiles*, 1, 28.

[13] John 15:5.

[14] Ephesians 3:14–15.

[15] J. Scott Lidgett, *The Fatherhood of God in Christian Truth and Life* (Edinburgh: T. & T. Clark, 1902), 39.

[16] *Donum vitae* [Instruction on Respect for Human Life in its Origin and on the Dignity of Procreation, Replies to Certain Question of the Day], Congregation for the Doctrine of the Faith (February 22, 1987), 5, II, A.

[17] US Census Bureau (2011).

[18] "The Family Creates the Peace of the Human Family," XXVII World Day of Peace (Vatican: December 8, 1993), 4.

[19] Genesis 1:27–28.

[20] Joseph MacDowell and Thomas Williams, *In Search of Certainty: Is There Any Such Thing as Truth? If So, Can We Know It?* (Wheaton, IL: Tyndale House Publication Inc., 2003), 26.

[21] Simone Weil, *Anthology*, ed. Sian Miles (New York: Grove Press, 1986), 202.

[22] Karol Wojtyla (John Paul II), *Love & Responsibility*, trans. H. T. Willetts (New York: Farrar, Straus and Giroux Inc., 1994), 227.

[23] Aquinas, *Summa theologica*, vol.1, q. 2, art. 3.

[24] Ibid.

[25] *Gaudium et spes* (December 7, 1965), 50.

[26] John Paul II, *Familiaris consortio*, 14.

[27] *CCC*, 2367 (cf. Eph. 3:14 and Mt. 23:9).

[28] Douglas Harper, "Online Etymology Dictionary," 2001–2012.

[29] Karol Wojtyla (John Paul II), *Love & Responsibility*, p. 248.

[30] John Paul II, *The Theology of the Body*, "Human Love in the Divine Plan" (Boston: Pauline Books & Media, 1997), 60.

[31] Sheen, *The World's First Love: Mary, Mother of God* (San Francisco: Ignatius Press, 1996), 147.

[32] John Paul II, *Gratissimam sane* [Letter to Family] (February 2, 1994), 9.

[33] John Paul II, *Familiaris consortio*, 25.

[34] John 3:27.

[35] Matthew 16:25.

[36] John Paul II, *Mulieris dignitatem* [Apostolic Letter], 8.

[37] 2 Peter 1:21.

[38] Genesis 2:18, 21–24. Saint Thomas Aquinas elaborated more on the contextual use of the word *helper* to mean *suitable partner*

in *Summa theologica*, vol. 1, pt. 1, q. 92, art. 1: "As a helper to man; not indeed as a helpmate in other works, as some say man can be efficiently helped by another Man, in other works; but as helper in the work of generation."

[39] John Paul II, *The Theology of the Body*, "Human Love in the Divine Plan" (Boston: Pauline Books & Media, 1997), 44.

[40] John Paul II, *Gratissimam sane*, 6.

[41] John Paul II, *The Theology of the Body*, 45.

[42] Joseph Cardinal Ratzinger and Angelo Amato, SDB, "Letter to the Bishops of the Catholic Church on the Collaboration of Men and Women in the Church and in the World," Congregation of the Doctrine of Faith (May 31, 2004), 6.

[43] CCC, 2331.

[44] Karol Wojtyla (John Paul II), *Love & Responsibility*, p. 2.

[45] "Letter of Pope John Paul II to Women" (June 29, 1995), 7.

[46] John Paul II, *Mulieris dignitatem*, 18.

[47] John W. Miller, *Calling God Father* (New York and Mahwah, NJ: Paulist Press), 117

[48] Lewis Yablonsky, *Father & Sons* (New York: Gardner Press Trade Book Company, 1990), 134.

[49] *New Oxford American Dictionary.*

[50] Saint Thomas Aquinas, *Summa theologica*, vol. 3, pt. 2, q. 119, art. 1.

[51] John Paul II, *Dives in misericordia* (November 30, 1980), 6.

[52] Aquinas, *Summa theologica*, vol. 1, q. 3, art. 3.

[53] John Paul II, *Dives in misericordia*, 6.

[54] Ibid.

[55] Ibid.

[56] David G. Benner, *Surrender to Love* (Downer Grove, IL: Intervarsity Press, 2003), 60.

[57] *New Oxford American Dictionary.*

[58] Sheen, *World's First Love*. The following is from page 158: "God loves man even in his sin. But He would not intrude upon human nature with His Love. So He woos one of the creatures to detach herself by an act of the will, from sinful humanity and to attach herself to Him so intimately that she might give Him human nature to begin the new humanity."

[59] Ibid.

[60] Benner, *Surrender to Love*, 59.

[61] Sheen, *World's First Love*, 159.

[62] Benedict XVI, *Solemnity of the Nativity of the Lord (homily)*. Vatican Basilica, Saturday, 24 December 2005.

[63] Saint Thomas Aquinas, *Questiones disputatae de malo*, 6, 1, 13.

[64] "Illusion of Ego," Inner Frontier: Cultivating Spiritual Presence. http://www.innerfrontier.org/Practices/IllusionOfEgo.htm. (accessed March 15, 2013).

[65] Sheen, *World's First Love*, 160.

[66] Anthony De Mello, *Walking on Water*, trans. Philip Berryman (New York: Crossroad Publishing Company), 96.

[67] Ibid., 89.

[68] Sheen, *World's First Love*, 164.

[69] Benner, *Surrender to Love*, 23.

[70] J. G. Paterson and L. T. Zderad, *Humanistic Nursing* (New York: John Willey & Sons, 1976), 132.

[71] Martin Buber, *I and Thou*, trans. Ronald G. Smith (New York: Macmillan Pub. Co., 1970).

[72] John Paul II, *Gratissimam Sane*, 11.

[73] International Theological Commission, "Communion and Stewardship: Human Persons Created in the Image of God," Saint Augustine's Confession, 1, 1, 1 (2000), 59.

[74] Ibid.

[75] Matthew 20:26

[76] Robert K. Greenleaf, *The Servant as Leader* (Westfield, IN: The Greenleaf Center for Servant Leadership, 2008).

[77] Robert K. Greenleaf, *Servant Leadership: A Journey into the Nature of Legitimate Power and Greatness* (New York: Paulist Press, 1977), 8.

[78] William Barclay, *Gospel of Mark* (Louisville, KY: Westminster John Knox Press, 2001), 298–299.

[79] Simone Weil, *"Gravity & Grace,"* Introductions by Gustave Thibon and Thomas R. Nevin (Bison book edition by the University if Nebraska Press, 1997), 182.

[80] Weil, *Anthology*, 208.

[81] John Paul II, *In my Own Words*, compiled by Anthony F. Chiffolo (New York: Gramercy Books, 1998), 48.

[82] John Paul II, *Centesimus annus* (May 1, 1991), IV, 41.

[83] William Barclay, *The Gospel of John* (Louisville, KY: Westminster John Knox Press, 2001), vol. 2, p. 6.

[84] Saint Thomas Aquinas, *Commentary on Pseudo-Dionysius on the Divine Names* (in div. nom.), 4, 4.

[85] Greenleaf, *Servant Leadership*, 21.

[86] Richard Rohr, *Falling Upward: Spirituality for the Two Halves of Life* (San Francisco: Jossey-Bass, 2011), xxii.

[87] De Mello, *Walking on Water*, 87.

[88] *Donum vitae*, 5, II, A.

[89] Benedict XVI, *Apostolic Journey of His Holiness to Valencia*, Vigil of Prayers on Occasion of the Fifth World Meeting of Families, City of Arts and Sciences, July 8, 2006.

[90] Vatican Council II, *Gaudium et spes*, Pastoral Constitution on the Church in the Modern World (December 7, 1965), 48, 1.

[91] CCC, 2384.

[82] Ibid., 2383 (cf. Canon Law 1153).

[93] Ibid., 2385.

[94] Ibid., 2366.

[95] Benedict XVI, *Address to participants in an International Congress Organized by Pope John Paul II Institution for Studies on Marriage and Family*. Clementine Hall, Rome, Italy (April 5, 2008).

[96] John Paul II, The Third World Meeting with Families: For the Occasion of Jubilee of Families, October 14, 2000, 5.

[97] John Paul II, *Code of Canon Law* [*Codex iuris canonici*], Latin–English edition (Washington, DC: Canon Law Society of America, 1983, 1999), 1,141. The full quotation in Latin is as follows: "*Matrimonium ratum et consummatum nulla humana potestate nullaque causa, praeterquam morte, dissolvi potest.*"

[98] Ibid., 1153, §1.

[99] Elizabeth Marquardt, "Ministering to Children of Divorce throughout Their Lives," Ministry Matters, January 2 2011..

[100] John Paul II, *Gratissimam sane*, 9.

[101] Vatican Council II, *Gaudium et spes*, 50.

[102] John Paul II, "God's Fatherhood is Basis of the Family," address to the fourteenth Plenary Assembly of the Pontifical Council for the Family, June 4, 1999.

[103] Marquardt, "Ministering to Children."

[104] Acts 1:20.

[105] Marquardt, "Ministering to Children."

[106] CCC, 2383 (cf. Canon Law, 1151–1155).

[107] John Paul II, *Gratissimam sane,* 12.

[108] Pontifical Council for the Family, "Children: Springtime of the Family and Society," Jubilee Families, Rome, October 14–15, 2000.

[109] Vincent Lindgren, *"Effects of Marital Discord on Children."* http://www.lindgrenmt.com/children.htm (accessed 24, January 2013)

[110] Pope Leo the Great, *Sermon on the Nativity* 21, n. 2

[111] Psalms 105:8–11.

[112] Benedict XVI, *Apostolic Journey to Valencia on the occasion of the fifth world meeting of families.* July 9, 2006.

[113] Benedict XVI, *Address to participants in an International Congress Organized by Pope John Paul II Institution for Studies on Marriage and Family.* Clementine Hall, Rome, Italy (April 5, 2008).

[114] Clarissa Pinkola Estés, "Women Who Run With the Wolves: Myth and Stories of the Wild Woman Archetype," (Ballantine Books, Nov. 27, 1996), 371.

[115] Archbishop Desmond Tutu, "Talk on Forgiveness," The Forgiveness Project, March 29, 2010, http://www.theforgivenessproject.com.

[116] International Theological Commission, "The Church and the Fault of the Past," December 1999, 5.1.

[117] Aquinas, *Summa contra gentiles,* q. 3, ch. 21.

[118] Hans Urs von Balthasar, ed., *Origen: Spirit & Fire,* trans. Robert J. Daly, SJ (Washington, DC: The Catholic University of American Press, 1984), p. 56, #75.

[119] Aquinas, *Questiones disputatae,* 20, 4.

[120] Daniel Landinsky, trans., *To See As God Sees: Love Poems from God; Twelve Sacred Voices from the East and West* (New York: Penguin Compass Group, 2002), 120.

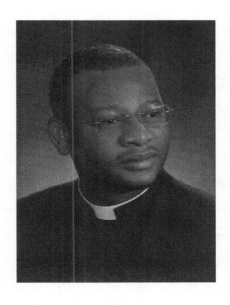

Fr. Faustinus Anyamele is a Catholic priest of the Archdiocese of Denver, Colorado. He received a B.A. in Philosophy from Pontifical Urbaniana University in Rome, Italy (1998), a B.A. in Sacred Theology from Pontifical Lateran University in Rome, Italy (2006) and M.A. in Divinity from St John Vianney Theological Seminary in Denver, Colorado USA (2006). Since his ordination, Fr. Faustinus has ministered in numerous parishes. He has been active teaching the Catholic faith, conducting the Faith Dialogue Series and giving talks/seminars. Fr. Faustinus has extensive experience in pastoral ministry with families, married couples, youth and young children. He is presently ministering at St Mary Catholic Parish, in Greeley, Colorado.

Fr. Faustinus incorporates detailed evidence and anecdotes to clearly articulate how so many innocent children today have been silently subjected to a profound psychological and emotional despair born of the absence of a true father figure in their lives. Growing up in dysfunctional families, some children suffer the adverse effects of separation or divorce and/or from the profound misunderstanding of the role and true concept of human fatherhood as a divine vocation that nurtures new human life. Many children have been denied their inalienable right to *a true father presence even* in *a presumed functional family.*

The purpose of this book is to guide fathers back to the true and original purpose of their fatherhood so that they may recapture once more the essence of true fatherhood as a vocation. Fatherhood is presented in the context of a Christian perspective and understood as complementary to motherhood in nurturing new life, which is a gift of God.

The book's thesis is clearly presented: fathers will be most effective and of greatest benefit to their children when they understand and embrace the idea that human fatherhood is a reflection of divine Fatherhood.

Made in the USA
San Bernardino, CA
08 May 2019